CONCILIUM

concilium 1999/2

FRONTIER VIOLATIONS: THE BEGINNINGS OF NEW IDENTITIES

Edited by

Felix Wilfred and
Oscar Beozzo

SCM Press · London
Orbis Books · Maryknoll

Published by SCM Press, 9–17 St Albans Place, London N1
and by Orbis Books, Maryknoll, NY 10545

Copyright Stichting Concilium
English translations © 1999 SCM-Canterbury Press Ltd and Orbis Books,
Maryknoll

ISBN: 0 334 03053 6 (UK)
ISBN: 1 57075 226 5 (USA)

Typeset at The Spartan Press Ltd, Lymington, Hants
Printed by Biddles Ltd, Guildford and King's Lynn

Concilium Published February, April, June, October, December.

Contents

Introduction: The Art of Negotiating the Frontiers

Felix Wilfred

Never before has history known so many frontiers as in our contemporary world, and at no period has there been such a frequent violation of frontiers as happens today. The establishment and removal of frontiers is the order of the day. This contradictory process is a window to the plight of humanity in these times in a dialectical tension between demarcation of particular identities – geographical, national, linguistic, cultural, ethnic, disciplinary, generic (genre) and so on – and crossing over to the other shore. If the consolidation of frontiers is characterized as ethnicity, tribalism, nationalism, etc., the crossing of them is known as globalism, multiculturalism, transnationalism, etc.

Ambiguities and contradictions

We are struck by the *ambiguity* of the phenomenon of frontier crossing. Crossing over could mean a march of aggression that infringes upon the freedom and autonomy of the realm invaded. It could be overt and violent, as when a power intrudes into the territory – physical, cultural, spiritual, etc. – of the other, as in the case of colonization of various kinds; or it could be covert and subtle, nevertheless destructive, as in the transnationalization of capital and homogenization of cultures. Ambiguity also marks the claims and advocacy regarding the affirmation and negation of frontiers. The most obvious example is the economic philosophy that calls for the lifting of all frontiers, so that capital and market may enter and play their imperial games unhindered, and at the same time the imposition of severe restrictions on the movement of the labour-force, the call to open the market of the South in the name of noble sentiments like a global world, while issuing embargoes and economic *fatwas* against the crossing of goods from the South.

The new at the fringes

The violation of frontiers is often a matter of *creativity*. It is this aspect of the issue which offers great hope for the emergence of refreshing new identities and the envisioning of alternatives. To be able to cross over, one has to locate oneself at the margins or at the edges of the present identity. To position oneself at the frontier is to adopt a very advantageous standpoint inasmuch as one can assess one's identity in a very creative and critical way. There is a great epistemological potential in being at the periphery, where the view of things is bound to be quite different from a centre where one may not understand what it means to come face to face with another identity, another spiritual, disciplinary, cultural or religious territory. It is interesting to note that, from another angle, anthropologists like Victor Turner and Arnold van Gennep have explored the critical and crucial importance of liminality or the border-stage of passage in the human life-cycle from one state to another. This is a moment of a fresh identity-formation, as in the case of crossing the threshold of puberty to step into the world of adulthood.

Creative violations

Certain aspects of crossing the frontiers are illustrated by the phenomenon of how *new genres* come into existence in literature. The history of literature is replete with writings which broke the frame of conventional classifications and violated the prescribed canons to found a new genre with a new identity of its own. We may recall here *The Waste Land* by T. S. Eliot or *The Name of the Rose* by Umberto Eco – the kind of writings that elude established parameters. A refusal to conform to firmly entrenched boundaries (patriarchalism, for example) has triggered off new forms and identities, as revealed, for instance, in contemporary feminist writings. In the various disciplines, too, the most creative works are today being done by scholars who challenge the conventional disciplinary frontiers, place themselves at the interstices and explore territories across the frontiers. Coming to everyday life, jumping over the endogamous caste-barricade to find a life-partner, is an act of defiance to the conventional social orthodoxy in a caste-hierarchical society. But often it is such acts of defiance that bring forth something new and set themselves up as a pattern for the shape of the things to come. Interracial or inter-ethnic unions engender an unprecedented physical and cultural identity, as is the case, for instance, in the phenomenon of mestizaje.

We may recall here another type of defiant frontier associated with the archetypal figure of Prometheus. By making available to humanity the fire from which it was excluded by Zeus, he also bridges the gulf between the human and the divine spheres. The Promethean violation of frontiers is a symbol of resistance to the way of defining frontiers in such a way that it constitutes an act of exclusion – exclusion from community, power, participation and so on. Like naming, frontier marking is an act of power. The ones defining the frontiers, generally, are also the ruling ones. No wonder then, that frontier-markings are most often acts of negations. They deprive millions on our globe of their basic human dignity and rights and consign them to the abyss of misery, endemic poverty and starvation. Frontiers are erected by the powers-that-be with the support of ideological armoury. A case in point is the relationship of the North to the South. But happily the various economic and trade barriers erected by the North and the ideologies attendant on them are audaciously challenged by many a Prometheus in the nations of the South.

Sojourn in different terrains and exile

It is important to note that the crossing of frontiers and the birth of the new are – as in the case of literature and academic disciplines – a sheer necessity for a new historical period or a particular context. The reality outgrows the bounds and frames in which it was set up and forces the crossing of frontiers and the breaking of the frame. It is followed be a re-mapping of the territory and a re-drawing of the frontiers. It may also result in a situation of sojourn in many territories at the same time for courageous explorations. Frontier violations and especially the attempt to dwell in many territories may shock the sensibilities of those accustomed to conventional borders. There is often a risk in being at the frontier and in crossing it, but such a risk is worth taking in view of the freedom and creativity it implies.

Frontier crossing, of course, is not simply an external event. It is also a spiritual experience. The inner dimension of frontier-crossing gets expressed vividly in the experience of exile. Exile is a harsh reality and at the same time a powerful metaphor that captures some of the poignant aspects of our contemporary life. Those finding themselves in the situation of exile are the ones who were forced to cross the frontiers, but who nurse in their hearts spiritual and nostalgic connections with the other side of the frontier. There is a sense of loss of what has been left behind, but what has been left behind continues to be deeply present in the exiled, shaping their innermost self and identity. Exile is also a state of mind that never gets accommodated to a forced situation – physical, intellectual, cultural, etc. – but lives by that inner strength and freedom which no closing of frontiers can smother. In this sense, there are many who are found in exile in their own lands.

Different postures towards frontiers

Finally, we need to also address the question of identities and frontier-crossing as a religious phenomenon. It is a fact that there are certain types of religions like Judaism, Christianity and Islam, for which frontiers and boundaries have greater significance than for people of primal religions or of other major religious traditions like Buddhism, Hinduism, Taoism, etc. In this context it is interesting to recall that, fluid and porous as its frontiers are, there is no proper definition of Hinduism, except in negative terms: a Hindu is someone who is not a Muslim, not a Christian, not a Sikh, not a Jain. This is obviously not the case with many other traditions, as they have their own prescribed definitions of inside and outside, orthodoxy and heterodoxy, and so on. The difference in attitude to frontiers in the different religious traditions evidently have consequences when it comes to dialogue among these religious traditions. The redeeming element in most religious traditions is the experience of mysticism. It is able to move and commune invisibly across the frontiers. Mysticism is a silent contestation to say that the frontiers are not impregnable and that there are other ways and means to reach out in spite of the visible religious fortifications.

Christianity and its shifting frontiers

The phenomena we observed and the reflections we made lead us to focus on Christianity in the crossing of frontiers. Contrary to the general impression, Christianity has re-drawn its own frontiers several times. This has always been a critical act at crucial times. I would highlight at least five such moments. The first crisis is connected with the times when the disciples of Jesus stood on the crossroads of forging their identity either as a sect within Judaism with strict Jewish membership and following its customs and traditions, or opening up the way of Jesus beyond the ethnic frontiers. What was achieved after much struggle was in fact a frontier-moving act. The widening of the circumference of the group led to the re-inventing of its identity. If the first re-drawing of frontiers was thus a matter of *ethnos* – overcoming the tendency of a reduction of Christianity within ethnical bounds – the second frontier-moving act had to do with the *chronos:* against the apocalyptic background of the imminent expectation of the Risen Christ, Christian discipleship was viewed as a matter for a brief period. A realization of the delayed parousia pushed the temporal frontiers of Christianity with very significant consequences. It paved the way not only for the consolidation of ecclesial structures providing for an indeterminate period, but also for shaping the Christian identity anew.

The third frontier-moving act was a matter of enlarging Christianity in such a way that its identity is not equated with the visible community but made to coincide with the realm of a mystery without borders. It is enough to recall here the *ecclesia ab Abel* of Augustine or, in modern times, the anonymous Christianity of Karl Rahner. The fourth is a case of contraction of the frontiers: it is the recognition that human reason has its own independent sphere, which is not to be confused with faith, and that temporal realities have their own autonomy free from the ecclesiastical power. The unfortunate experiences of attempting to extend ecclesiastical power over science and the claim of ecclesiastical authorities over the temporal sphere (the two-swords theory) forced the church to withdraw itself from certain territories and readjust its own frontiers. And this, once again, could not fail to have implications for th identity and shape of Christianity. Fifthly, in recent decades, a re-adjustment of frontiers among the churches within Christianity has also taken place. The rigidity of frontiers gave room for a more flexible understanding when Vatican II employed the significant expression that the church of Jesus Christ *subsists* in the Catholic Church. It was another clear case of a fresh discovery of ecclesial identity.

The story is not over. The new millennium will see many more shiftings of frontiers, with far-reaching consequences for the construction of the self-identity of Christianity. A very crucial question that faces Christianity today is again a question of frontiers. It is the question of the frontiers with other religious traditions. It is certainly going to occupy our attention in the first decades of the new century. But as I observed in my article in the first number of *Concilium* this year, the question of frontiers may not be resolved by concluding the present debate between inclusivism and pluralism. It calls for something more. And that leads me to the next two points.

The art of negotiating frontiers: the challenge of the new century

The crossing of frontiers is a larger human experience and is not only a matter of religious frontiers. An open church willing to relate to the world, the larger society and many types of identities will increasingly face the question how to go about the reality of frontiers. It is the modern version of the question of love of neighbour, constitutive of which is the recognition of the other's self-identity: individual, collective, cultural, etc. So also, the traditional Christian motive of reconciliation has to express itself today in the way we face the question of frontiers and boundaries and how we cross over and reach out to the other in her or his otherness.

In a general cultural environment in which Christians experience many frontiers being reinforced and others collapsing, and still others meeting and merging, the need of the time is to develop the spiritual agility and wisdom to deal with frontiers and boundaries. Here theology has a very innovative role to play. I mean to say that theology cannot develop the relationship with other identities by simply sharpening its conceptual and dialectical tools, but needs to cultivate the art of negotiating the frontiers. The inculcation of this art should become part of the culture and pedagogy within Christianity. It amounts to an education of the Christians and Christian communities to the true spirit of universality. By negotiating the frontiers and communing across them, Christians will continuously discover new dimensions of their own faith-identity. The experimental and open-ended character inherent in every frontier-crossing and encounter will lead us to perceive our faith-identity ever afresh. Much of the Christian future lies on the periphery, in the frontier-zones. Encounter with new identities need not signify a threat to a church that understands itself as universal because it is a communion in difference. What is the universality of Christianity if it does not become an attitude and way of life that characterize the life and spirit of Christians?

Crossing the frontiers between Being and nothingness: towards a new millennium

The art of crossing the frontiers needs to be rooted and inspired by something much deeper. If Being and nothingness are the ultimate metaphysical (*pace* postmodernists) polarities, this needs to get reflected in any fuller understanding and approach to frontiers. One needs to learn to cross the frontier both from the pole of Being or fullness and from the pole of nothingness. In the Indic civilization these two approaches are represented by the Vedic and Upanishadic tradition of *puranam* (fullness) on the one hand, and of *sunyata* (nothingness) of Buddhism on the other. The ability to cross only from one of these can severely handicap the enterprise and weaken our understanding of the world, the Ultimate and the self. The Christian attempts to cross over to the other, to the different, has been by and large from the pole of being or fullness. This naturally creates problems, which can be overcome by activating the ability also to cross over from the pole of nothingness or emptiness. The central Christian mystery of Jesus Christ offers the revelation of both fullness and nothingness – the total self-emptying. Many frontiers which are found difficult to negotiate and cross over could be crossed by making use of the other pole represented in the Christian mystery of emptiness as self-abnegation, so as to reach a deeper perception of the mystery of God, the world and the self. Perhaps here lies something that could become an important programme for Christianity and its theology at the turn of the new millennium.

I · The Phenomenon

Human Beings Cross Frontiers

Yves Cattin

Human existence establishes itself and re-establishes itself in a kind of insurmountable paradox because that is inherent in it. To be real, and not just imaginary, this existence must recognize its limits, accept them and claim them. But if it is to be human, this same existence must constantly reject these limits and try to live beyond them. Human beings are neither angels nor beasts, said Pascal, but the intermediate status which he assigned to them can only really be lived out if human beings hold on to both their animal nature and their spirituality: they have to persist in acting as angels without ever renouncing the beast in them; they have to be ready to exist as a corporeal soul or a spiritual body. It is here that the inherent nature and fullness of human existence is to be found, in that corporeal spirit which language is never adequate for naming. For here the adjectival epithet 'corporeal' is a noun of the noun 'soul' at the same time as soul is the adjective of the adjective. The soul is body and the body is soul, indissolubly and substantially.

This unity is as it were the mark of the finitude of all human existence. This existence, in so far as it is spiritual, is finite because it is corporeal. This statement must not be understood in the sense of classical dualism, which thinks that the soul is in the body like the content in a container, like the water in the vase which stops it spreading. On the contrary, as Thomas Aquinas affirms in a magnificent text: 'the soul is in the body as a container and not as contained by it'.[1] It is not the soul or the spirit that is in the body, but it is the body that is in the soul. And in order to exist, the soul makes the body arise out of itself and then manifests itself as a human soul. The body is the limit of the soul; it is the first frontier which allows people to establish themselves in a concrete worldly existence and which they must cross to go to the world and to others. So the body is that ontological impotence which prevents the human spirit from presenting itself as pure and absolute spirit. And in being human, the body is an essential quality of the soul.

I. The first frontier

1. The inherent experience of the body

To rediscover the inherent experience of the body it is necessary to abandon the dualistic dialectic of the body and the spirit or the soul, the outside and the inside, which has been part of all cultural practices and philosophical or theological reflections, in order to rediscover a forgotten experience, that of the original totality that we are. The spirit and the body are not two realities of which we are composed in a way which is difficult to maintain. The body and the spirit are just two words, two ways of speaking of human beings. If we try to keep these words, we need to make it clear that in using them in turn we mean to say that if human beings are to exist in a human way, they must develop in two directions: they must become the world by becoming the body, and they must become themselves by becoming spirit. Here the first becoming conditions the second.

Human beings appear as, and are, completely body, in that they come to the world and appropriate it for themselves. And they appear as, and are, entirely spirit or soul in that in this very movement of appropriating the world they manifest themselves as a presence of themselves to themselves, a presence in the face of the world. Thus human beings never exist in the pure identity of the self to the self, but are always a mediation of themselves to themselves which goes through the body. To come to themselves, human beings come to the world. And the body signifies that the humanity of human beings is always engaged in this movement of going to the world and returning to oneself, in passing towards the other than oneself in order to become and be oneself. Thus exile and migration would seem to be the movement basic to the humanity of every human being. Human beings have to abandon and depart from their being in order to become guests of the world and thus regather themselves in the fullness of their regained being. Thomas Aquinas calls this movement *redditio in se completa*.

2. The body as limit and as frontier

Thus the body is in the soul; it is the soul in giving itself to exist as a human soul; and it manifests itself as the limit of the soul and the spirit. This word 'limit' must be understood properly. The limit is what determines the space required for a being to be able to exist as a being in the world, as this being is in itself, determined and limited. But the limit is also what prevents this being from going beyond what it is, what makes it only what it is. Philosophers will say that the limit, here the body, is the mark of the finitude of the being, that which signifies that the spirit is a human spirit. But this limit and this frontier are also what has to be crossed in order to come to the world, for a human being to set out to exist in the face of the world. When the spirit produces its body it invents space, it constructs the world in a basic gesture, the matrix of all the architectures of the world: both this internal architecture which we call the construction of the personality and the material architectures in which we live and which we see.

The body is this original architecture. It is this space with its limits and its frontiers, its vital centres, its defences and its weaknesses. Certainly in the imagination, but also in experience, the body is a complex and hierarchical space which is invested both within by the subject which 'occupies it' and outside by others who look at it, approach it and touch it. The body is this first and original territory of humanity, at the origin of all territories and all geographies.

That is what happens when I come into the world, whether at my birth or in each of my daily actions. I come into the world, I make myself body in a certain way; I am of the world. But in this very act, I come into the world by presenting myself to the world. Then I am not of the world but I am faced with it, and face it. Thus the body is always orientated, it offers and imposes the 'here' of its presence and the 'elsewhere' of its absence, what is before it, on its right and left. Thus as soon as the spirit manifests itself as body, it 'geometrizes' the world; it goes through the world, 'surveying' it in every sense; and it orientates the world by orientating itself in it. What we call the world is only the projection, in an infinite straight line which in fact is always limited, of the structural geography of my body, the network of all the courses taken by body, real and possible. Thus the world is always the world and at the same time my world. The world is my body, as a virtual part of it, and my body exists only by occupying the world, by being preoccupied with it, by being concerned for it, and by feeding on the flesh of the world.

3. Migrant human beings 'renting' the world

So human beings are migrants: they ceaselessly cross and recross the frontiers of their bodies in order to go to what is not themselves and in order to become themselves. In this migration, human beings invent space, namely the place of their presence, the place where they present themselves by representing themselves. The coming of human beings to themselves is thus the coming of human beings to the world and the coming of the world to them.

Here we should not talk of space in general, which is only an empty space, i.e. a word, but rather of human spaces, which are so many modes of our presence in the world. One can then distinguish an existential space, which is the cluster of networks of all the courses taken by my body and its temporary abodes. My goings and comings in the world that I appropriate for myself mark out a kind of personal geography which is the trace left both by my body and by my freedom. It can then be called abstract space, to denote the most extended network of all the possibilities of my body. This space is both the objective limit of my real existential space and also that to which it is potentially open. It is like the extension of this space. That means that I am never the prisoner of my space: I am here, but I can always go and be elsewhere. This space which I call 'abstract' here, and which should perhaps be called 'virtual' in the sense of a 'figure of my power', is like the dotted trace of all my futures. 'Elsewhere' is then the name of a future. Finally, these existential and abstract (or virtual) spaces are possible only because I exist within limits and the 'elsewheres' of which I dream always reveal themselves to experience as narrowly limited 'heres'. But whatever these 'here-elsewheres' that I inhabit may be, there is always an 'elsewhere' of which I can dream. It is sometimes said of someone that 'he is never nowhere'. The 'here' which I inhabit always relates to an 'everywhere here', to a totality of space, an infinity of space that my body invests as total presence in the world.

Thus human beings always 'rent' space; they realize their humanity in a concrete way only by inventing space as a place of being and existing. This 'renting' is always a multiple or plural 'renting': the always unfinished effectuation of the body as a concrete possibility of a world. And this 'multiple renting' can only take place against the dreamed-of horizon of a 'total renting' of the world, in the impossible but necessary dream of inhabiting the totality of the world. Then the body, my body, by deploying its existence, deploys space before it and invents its places as the retreats and traces of its desire.

4. *The places of human beings*

It is necessary to describe these places of human beings, since they teach us about the basic migrations of the humanity of every human being.[2] Certainly this place is first of all a place, a space of one's own, where one's body can develop its potential, in other words a place where one can be oneself and become oneself. The body gathers itself within the limits which it gives itself and which it assumes (or which one gives it and imposes on it), and it affirms itself as 'me', as body-spirit. This 'deposition' of the body as myself ranges from the space where I work intellectually, where I am spirit, to the space where I am only a body asleep in the bedroom. Each time the space is structured to serve the bodily/spiritual expression that is required of it. The place is then like the name I bear, the face which is mine: it is the limited space which circumscribes my personal identity, such as I give myself by delimiting it. This place of identity is like the visible body of the person.

But this place that is here said to form identity is always an open place which makes possible the dynamic identity that I am always in process of shaping and giving to myself. For 'becoming myself' is possible and becomes effective only if the self is not enclosed, in a place which would be a prison; if the self can 'pass' to otherness, and encounter the other than me. Also, instead of speaking of a 'place of identity', it would be better to speak of a 'place of identification', a place with quite fixed and quite mobile limits, of such a kind that it can 'contain' the infinities of my successive identifications. This place of identification is also and at the same time a relational place, open to the possibility of the other who comes to me, and more generally to the whole world. Thus the house is a place of self-recollection, of the recollection of the self by the self and with the self, but it is also a place of welcome, of openness to the guest who comes and whom I receive. In this sense it is always cosmos, world or microcosm, the place of all places, a place which gathers and assembles the different places that one goes through one after the other. It would be easy to show, in the analysis of both the most private and the most public places, how in these places this dialectic of the identical and the relational is put into action. The room in which I sleep, the bed on which I rest, are the places to which I withdraw in the greatest solitude, apart from the world and its noise. But they are also the places where I make love, in other words where I realize the highest relationship with another by bringing about the birth of the world. And even when the other and the world are not present there physically, they still return to haunt these places in dreams or nightmares. At the opposite extreme, if it is authentically to be a place, the most public place where I realize my being-with-others needs to be such a place that I can always be there and remain myself there.

In this place of their own, where human beings establish themselves and construct their personal identity, openness and obligation to the other are even more profound. For in this place men and women not only welcome other men and women and the world, but also welcome and gather the whole history of humanity. This is a historical place, a place which signifies my history and the history of all men and women by gathering up its traces. Here the word 'historical' is to be understood in the basic sense that my body, the body of my self, is always a historical body, and that the place of my body gathers up spatially the traces of this history, even if only partially and provisionally. Because it is historical, the place is a gathering together of the totality of a past which is definitively over and which exists only in this chance, transitory point that is the present state of the place. Thus the place of human beings always recalls these human beings, at the same time as it presents itself as a monument of humanity, as legible and as indecipherable as any monument. These remarks can be summed up in the statement that the place is always a memory or memorial in the basic sense of the spatial inscription of a human past which authorizes and opens up a future for humankind.

In inventing the place, human beings invent a place for being themselves, for becoming themselves, and a place for being together. Then it is possible to realize what is called the encounter, the communication or the society, in other words a limitation of space and time, and in this space-time words, gestures and silences. Thus by inventing and occupying their places, human beings draw a provisional and complex geography of diverse and multiple humanities which are both distinct and always interconnected.

II. The frontier and the bridge

1. Human beings as nomads

That is possible only because there are limits which authorize a personal or collective identification and because these limits are constantly exceeded in every direction in a perpetual and paradoxical movement of appropriation and disappropriation, in a constant conveyance and exchange of humanities.

Thus humanity is always a nomad humanity and it gathers and disperses in human places as an immense story, an endless history. In the same way written narratives, in the form of myths and legends, cross and organize groups, individuals and their places by distinguishing them and binding them together, by making phrases and itineraries.

Then the individuals or the groups shift by obeying a kind of spatial syntax. Then they obey codes which order and control their conduct, which regulate changes in space by putting places in linear or interwoven series. These places are then linked in a more or less closed or easy way by 'modalities' which specify the kind of transition from the one to the other. But always limits are encountered and frontiers are crossed and re-crossed.

2. Abstract humanity in its frontiers

How are we to analyse this nomadism of human beings, individuals or groups, this practice of human places and spaces which are practices of humanity? Here it has to be said that over long centuries human beings have been content to go, to travel, to occupy places by sharing them out, sometimes disputing over them. Humanity has invented or followed trajectories, whether spontaneous or compulsory, from the near to the far, which then becomes near. History recounts these journeys with their landmarks, their milestones and their limits. It tells us how such human ventures have been possible along with the whole chain of operations required in this uninterrupted adventure of encounters, wars and interbreeding. Thus history reveals a spontaneous and unconsidered order in humankind.

But our modernity has slowly imposed a new rigour and rationalization which we see at work both in the emergence of nationalities and in the new concern given to the individual; this has been put into a legal space which is becoming increasingly precise and well-defined. Little by little, maps of humanity have been developed and imposed which materialize and authorize the courses that can be taken by humanity, and human beings have allowed themselves to be shut up in these abstract geographies.

Little by little, the humanities of human beings have been inscribed and circumscribed within material and spiritual frontiers, and as this is done men and women are solidified and so to speak fixed, so that they forget the possibility of change. Then frontiers which were crossing points have become barriers. In forgetting the spontaneous movements in life, these humanities have become abstract, defined and definable by the right of blood and soil.

3. The frontier

Whatever this development may have been, even if the humanity of human beings is barricaded within more or less well guarded frontiers, human beings have continued to move, to emigrate. And their itineraries, like the maps which are abstractions of them, are always obliged to state these limits and then to establish them. Human beings who go through space on different trajectories always establish and articulate it by marking out boundaries, in other words by inventing limits or frontiers for more or less extended cultural areas. Like animals, human beings mark out their territory or territories. They constantly form spaces by checking, confronting and shifting frontiers.

It is this demarcation, this partition of space, which makes it a structured space, and it is the establishment of frontiers which organizes spatiality. By being given structure in this way, space becomes hostile and inhuman; then the individual or the group regresses towards the disturbing and fatalistic experience of an unshaped, indistinct, nocturnal totality and is lost. And before all else, this space structured by limits (walls, river, stream, forest, mountain, etc.) is spoken: it is put into words, into stories which become legal and administrative.

The essential function of frontiers is to 'humanize' the nomadism of individuals and human groups, which could then be compared with the transhumance of animals. In fact, the frontiers introduce a rule of humanity into this animal transhumance. They authorize or prohibit movements; they orientate them. As a rule they are the basis for the circulation of humanity and interchanges within it. Consequently every frontier is always coupled with a bridge, a crossing point, which authorizes or prohibits traffic.

The limit imposed by the frontier first of all has the function of authorizing, opening up a space, a theatre of action. In this delimited space conduct is commanded and authorized by the *ius*, law. Without this delimitation, conduct would become uncertain, perilous, fatal. Thus a place is, as the Romans said, propitious or unpropitious, depending on whether or not it gives human action this necessary foundation of delimited space. In this connection we might reflect on the Roman ritual of the declaration of war on a foreign people or even the act of alliance. This rite is performed by a cast of specialized priests, the *fetiales*, and consists of a march in three stages. The first is to the threshold of the frontier, but within Roman territory; the second is at the frontier itself, and the third is beyond the frontier, in foreign lands. The aim of this rite was to make the space propitious, lucky, by appropriating it; once it had been performed, the war or the alliance could begin, in an established and claimed humanity. The rite opens up space and gives a setting for human actions; thus the space is spoken of and told of before being crossed. The frontiers open up a field which authorizes social practices.

4. *The bridge, or the crossing of the frontier*

However, every frontier contains a contradiction, which is signified by the relationship between the frontier which delimits and 'legitimates' inner space and the bridge which makes it possible to cross the frontier to go to a foreign land, towards the world outside. The frontier delimits a human space only on condition that it can be opened up; otherwise this space becomes a prison.

So the frontier, which is a limit, is also a crossing point. That is the classical problem of the frontier: to whom does it belong? It is the space that it limits, but it is also the external area which comes to touch this space. So the frontier appears as a kind of theoretical non-place, and this contradiction can be removed only if the frontier offers mediation: it stops people, but it also lets them pass. Here separation is communication, and the frontier is the articulation of different but like humanities: it is passage, dialogue. And conflict develops only when the frontier ceases to play this role and becomes a wall that cannot be crossed.

The bridge over the river which materializes the frontier between two countries links one bank to another. It is the bridge that makes the banks, and at each of its entrances the bridge draws to itself the two banks and the two countries. Thus at a point in the river the bridge brings the lands together and makes a friendly world. The bridge allows the river to flow, it leaves it in its course, but it gives men and women a way over the river. It leaves the river as it is, but at the same time it annuls it, since instead of being a barrier which cannot be crossed, the river becomes a way. By performing this function the bridge brings together all the roads so that they become one road, and offers passage to the other bank, to other roads. Thus the bridge ceases to be something that has been built and becomes a place, a place which gives place, a place which makes a place, i.e. which produces a meeting-place for those who come to the bridge, a place which has been constructed, liberated: which breaks open the prison and thus brings freedom. Thus the bridge reveals the true sense of the banks of the river. Before the bridge existed they were prison walls. Each of them marked the end of a land ignorant of the land opposite. With the bridge the banks are still limits, but they are open limits: they free a country by opening it up to another country. It is still necessary for people to cross the bridge if that land is not to be a desert or a prison. Only then does the bridge link human habitations and different humanities, which become shared humanities, and thus richer and more human.[3]

We must conclude from these remarks that the frontier and the bridge are markers of the human condition. Human beings live in the places that they build and mark out: that is the only way for human beings to be human. The human being who has no place, the homeless person, is someone who has lost humanity. The house that I build and thus inhabit, the country in which I live, are thus a provocation to life, and a rejection of death, a protest against it. And the greatest danger which constantly threatens this house is that it may become a tomb or a public place, open to all the winds; the greatest danger that constantly threatens this country is that it may become a concentration camp or an endless and limitless space.

To live in a human way is thus to set up limits, to build walls, to establish frontiers. And to do that is to establish a freedom, a life; it is to cultivate a humanity. The establishment of this space is a pacification of space, and thus of human existence. To live in a human way is to let its being be; it is to safeguard this being by surrounding it with the protection of limits which are both limits of space and those of freedom. But these limits, these frontiers that we build, are always open to an 'elsewhere' to which we can go and which can come to us.

5. The obligation to offer hospitality

Because the frontier is always crossed by a bridge, because it is always the frontier that gives freedom, human beings always find themselves obliged to offer hospitality, to welcome otherness. The communities or the countries themselves are the hosts, and popular language is not wrong to speak of a welcoming house or country. The freedom which freedoms give is a freedom which must extend beyond them.

. Hospitality is the basic rule of the humanity of human beings and their humanization. But the obligation to offer hospitality which this exchange imposes on humanity is not undifferentiated. Like humanity itself, hospitality is subject to rules. What is exchanged between human beings is their 'being human' and not their lack of humanity or defective humanity. So hospitality is naturally a demand for humanity, both for those who receive and those who are received. It requires both of them to be more human and to renounce their defects, their inhumanity. Thus all hospitality is critical, going beyond all ethnocentricity. De jure and de facto this hospitality is 'infinite': it is a welcome not only to the friend and the neighbour next door, but also to the person from a long way off, the foreigner. It makes the one who approaches me my neighbour, even if he or she comes from the ends of the earth. Hospitality sets in motion processes of reciprocal knowledge and recognition. And by virtue of this, it is the first and last form of the respect for human beings and of human rights. It has this character first in a negative form, which consists in allowing others to exist, in opening up a place for them where they can show who they are. Then, positively, respect becomes the communion of our similarities; it becomes the invention, beyond the recognition and surmounting of our differences, of a place for living together humanly.

III. Human beings as strangers

1. Lost places

Today we are in a relatively new situation, which requires unprecedented imagination and thought of us. The frontiers seem to be disappearing, yet they are vigorously being claimed in the face of the strangers who press at our gates. Individuals are getting lost in the mass and the mass movements, yet they are claiming their independence and their originality. Places for encounter, i.e. for the social being of men and women, are becoming increasingly rare and harder and harder to discover. The cities are urbanized and colonized, apartments are standardized, streets and squares are routes or barricades and the countryside is waymarked and colonized by tourism and touristic activities.

Like spaces, so too times are becoming increasingly difficult to discover. The time in which we live is marked out as a grid by the diary, the clock or the watch, and one can no longer waste time, since 'time is money'. Even free time or liberated time is an empty time, and therefore boring, so people hasten to fill it with leisure activity. And like these free times, holiday times when one experiences sheer freedom, those gratuitous but vague spaces, like the churches, are progressively disappearing or are being deserted for useful times and spaces.

Thus without our noticing it, the places and times of life are becoming non-places of life, places through which one passes, in which one can no longer stop, take one's time, waste time. The places of which I have spoken are becoming places of transit, non-places of being.

2. The generalization of the non-place

It is no exaggeration to say that the places of life, the places where one can be said to reside, are disappearing. Places of birth are becoming unimportant, the simple mention of an abstract place on a civic document; that is all the more so nowadays, since people are born in non-places like clinics or maternity homes. From there individuals are as it were snatched up by non-places of life, where they only 'pass their lives'. They live in apartments, luxurious or wretched, places of temporary transit. They go to clubs or hotels, get into cars, drive around everywhere, always obeying the imperatives of employment in a generalized transhumance. Finally they die in hospitals, places of transit *par excellence*; they spend several hours or days in a mortuary and disappear into the incinerator. For this perpetual movement never ends, as it once did, in the rest of a cemetery and the peace of a cave, but in the smoke of the crematorium. These individual itineraries are taken over and facilitated by a dense network of transport all over the place, a network which means that in being somewhere, at some point, one is already possibly everywhere else, in any part of the world.

This description is hardly an exaggeration. Its sole aim is to indicate and to emphasize the movement in which we are all more or less caught up, and to draw attention to the progressive and perhaps inescapable disappearance of the places where human beings are, the places where they are themselves.

This development has numerous consequences and it would take time to analyse them. Here one can only make suggestions. The first is the most important. In this forgetfulness of places and this lostness in space without places, individuals lose their bodies and familiarity with their bodies. The body becomes a kind of strange alien, a heterogeneous and ostentatious object which delivers over the self, bound hand and foot, to the caprices of the social scene. Then people get lost in an undiffer-entiated space in which the indications, the marks which make it possible to distinguish the near from the far, disappear. The foreigner begins to proliferate everywhere and my next-door neighbour is no closer to me than the South Sea islander whom television broadcasts sometimes bring into my sitting room. The foreigner is present everywhere, invading us like a fantasy, because the foreigner is in us, is us. The extremist or racist movements are rooted in this fear. They defend a return to the values of the earth, the soil, roots, and reject foreigners as a threat to personal or national identity. But the fear and the rejection of the other which they develop are merely an expression of an anxiety about already being lost. We have become strangers to ourselves. In our modern societies, in which solitude and anonymity are becoming general, individuals become nonentities, and the only way of distinguishing between them in society is to give each of them a number in society. And all the numbers are the same. The person and the self disappear, swallowed up in a solitude which is a prelude to hell. For to be no one is to be without anyone. To be without oneself is to be without the other who recognizes one and calls one. And those who are no longer called become the individuals of a lost humanity.

3. The new human being

In these non-places, each individual develops a new and strange image of himself or herself, a kind of generalized dilution of the self, a dispersal to meet the demands of the story in which he or she is imprisoned. At times, this dilution of the self is concentrated at the control points of the system: the customs hall, the toll barrier, the till, the ticket machine. Then I become myself again, but this a self which is numbered, filed, anonymous and evaluated. I no longer have a real identity or real relations; on the contrary, I exist in a definitive solitude which is also a radical solitude, since like everyone else I exist in the same routes, the same codes, the same messages, the same concerns.

So for the individual there is no longer tradition or history; these are forgotten or put in brackets. What counts is the present movement, in the rush of events. Individuals only begin to exist when something happens, and the past is only evoked in allusions made in order to reinforce the present. Then individuals identify with what happens (not even something that happens to them) and with the image that they are given. Then a kind of generalized public narcissism takes place, in a closed circuit. I am this man or this woman who advertises for this car, sold in this supermarket, who praises this commercial radio station, who praises this supermarket, who praises this hotel, who praises this airline, who . . . And so on in an infinite circularity.

So the present situation is infinitely complex. We exist in a jumble of places and non-places. All our places of being are threatened by non-places, like houses which end up all looking like one another because they are furnished by Habitat or Ikea. And all the non-places that we visit dream of being true places, like the house in the country which one wants to be rooted in the earth, like the old farmhouse. Since we are always in transit, we dream of residing. We are constantly on the move and we are passengers, lost on the motorway junctions; we have forgotten what true journeys were like, with real meetings and real cross-roads. And everywhere we communicate, when we have even unlearned the words of our tongue, in a universal and utilitarian language: basic English, poor and standardized. Thus everywhere the humanity that we live out becomes a humanity which is spoken of and dreamed of.

IV. Conclusion

This new world is a network of networks in which all the routes are both identical and singular. Human beings as persons lose themselves in it and become anonymous individuals, identical and interchangeable. And in this world, place is no longer defined by a system of relations and oppositions to other places, like the town and its village. The countryside no longer belongs to these separate packagings of places: villages, cantons, departments, regions, and nations; and as human beings disappear, so too does what we call the world. Places lose their differences and their specific characteristics, and rootless human beings, without faith or law, become imaginary human beings.

To speak of the catastrophe which threatens us is not to say that it cannot be avoided. It is for us to claim a lively and thus a mortal life, to reinvent a birthplace which is new and unprecedented, a birthplace of human beings, for themselves, a place where each person can re-establish and maintain identity, where they can encounter the others and gather up time by leaving some trace. Consequently we also have to reinvent frontiers and bridges for crossing them, since we cannot keep the old frontiers and the old bridges. We must invent new forms of behaviour, new messages and new relationships. At the very moment when new technologies are making frontiers illusory, we risk succumbing to the evil 'impulse' or encasing the same frontiers in concrete in order to enclose and magnify our individual or collective particularities. In doing so we build on and fill the spaces between the clearways; we freeze places, we build 'blocks' and walls. In contrast to this, we have to learn or relearn a logic of ambiguity, not to forget that the door that shuts is the very door that opens, that frontiers are made to be crossed. So our essential and urgent task is to build 'bridges'. This is a difficult task, since while the bridge liberates people from imprisonment, there is a risk that it will destroy autonomy; if it unites insularities, there is a risk that it will set them against each other. The bridge that can be destructive as the point of departure for a conquering people or the invasion of barbarian strangers is also the structure which gives to all interiority the externality that it needs. It gives all humanity governed by norms its necessary otherness, thus signifying that human beings cannot live without their 'others'.

It is easy to deduce from this that limits and frontiers are made to be crossed; that they are mobile and must constantly shift, indefinitely inventing a new order of places. They are like the Greek statuettes called Kodora, the invention of which is attributed to Daedalus: they marked limits, but by constantly shifting they invented mobile places, in the image of the mobile humanities of humankind.

Translated by John Bowden

Notes

1. Thomas Aquinas, *Summa Theologiae* 1 a q.52 a.1.

2. For this description, I am making free comments on the categories proposed by Marc Auge in his work *Non Lieux. Introduction à une anthropologie de la modernité*, Paris 1992, 69ff.

3. To supplement these hasty and over-abstract analyses see the magnificent novel by Ivo Andrić, *The Bridge over the Drina*, London 1959, reissued 1995. The bridge which is the principal 'hero' of this novel plays precisely the role that I try to describe here, by putting two alien worlds in communication (or in opposition): the Turkish Ottoman empire and Christian Serbia or Austria.

Immigrants and Asylum Seekers: Signs of Globalization and a Question for Theology

Albert Bastenier

Globalization, a new component of modernity

What has come to be called 'globalization' clearly involves more than the transnational mobility of capital and the relocation of businesses. It equally involves the mobility and relocation of people and even entire populations. Under the imperative pressure of the market, and also from the current political somersaults of some of the former colonial countries, these are physically transplanted by migration or the quest for a humanitarian asylum.

This phenomenon is not totally new, since the beginning of migratory flows towards the industrialized countries dates back to the nineteenth century. However, some of these old tendencies have become so radical that they take on a new significance: the systematic intermixing of originally different populations ends up in a mass cosmopolitanism which adds a decisive multicultural component to the modernity of the host societies. Moreover this phenomenon of transplantation, like modernity itself, cannot be reduced to a logic which is simply economic. It is also political and cultural. Hence to think of human transplantations as one of the symbolic factors in globalization presupposes the articulation of these different logics.

First, the magnitude of the phenomenon should be noted. It is generally estimated that between sixty and seventy million people today live outside their country of origin. Whether in transit or in process of resettling, they are looking for better living conditions. Their displacement across frontiers can be explained by unequal development, natural catastrophes, wars, internal conflicts and political or religious repression. Between fifteen and twenty million of them invoke the right to asylum in justified fear of persecution and are thus political refugees in the terms of the United Nations Charter. All those who cross frontiers settle in a new context which often proves problematical. Their situation is analogous to that of which Marx spoke in the nineteenth century, referring to the proletariat: 'it camps in the midst of the nation without truly forming part of it'. So the question is that of their social belonging.

In the countries in which they arrive, these transplantations give rise to a new xenophobic unrest which is magnified by the mass media. This unrest stems from complex motivations, ranging from the spontaneous fear of newcomers whose culture is different to the fear of the consequences that they can represent for system of employment and social security. But among the 'old nations' of the northern hemisphere, that results above all in a neo-nationalism which Habermas calls 'the chauvinism of well-being'. This neo-chauvinism in fact revolves round the question of what either party expects the state to provide.

We need also to ask whether this polarization of relations between 'old nationals' and 'newcomers' does not bring in its wake a redefinition of the terms which denote social relations and belonging within these societies. For we cannot but be struck by the number of contemporary situations in which the cultural argument over language, shared traditions and religion is in process of becoming the decisive factor in the process of differentiation and the development of a social hierarchy between individuals and groups. Here it is parallel to the other factors which determine the construction of identity, like sex, age, class and nationality.

From this starting point we can better understand the unexpected but increasingly frequent use of the notion of 'ethnic minority' by the social sciences when they want to describe the dynamic of relations within modern societies. In fact it often seems that the famous topological distinction once made by F. Tönnies between 'community' and 'society', which had led almost all modern thinkers to accept the idea of the extinction of ethnic groupings, is no longer self-evident. Certainly, in the face of the universalism of reason characteristic of modernity, Kant emphasized the importance that would be attached to the subjective particularism of nationalisms in the world of war between the states. And Marx had grasped the power which would be shown by the antagonism of the subjective conscience of the classes in industrialized societies. However, neither could have foreseen the influence that cultural particularisms were going to show at the end of the twentieth century. Finally, there is the difficulty of thinking of social belonging on the basis of the apparently irreconcilable demands of universality and the singularities, which forms the current stumbling block in political philosophy within democratic societies that have become multicultural.

So, contrary to all expectations, the current experience would seem to be that the identification of the self and others on an ethnic and cultural basis is part of the fundamental and permanent register of social symbolism. This type of identification is even taking on a new relevance, in that it lends itself particularly well to the combination of economic, political and cultural interests which globalization is setting in motion. This constitutes an unexpected source of the formation of a social hierarchy among individuals and groups, and shapes the oppositions between them within modern societies.

The inadequacy of economics and politics

As is witnessed by the processes of the marginalization or the social exclusion of foreigners who have been transplanted by a globalization which is above all economic, we are witnessing the manifest incapacity of the single market to bring about sufficient integration in society. But as is shown by the rise of extremely right-wing populisms, we are also witnessing the impotence of the sphere of national state politics itself to perform this task of integration. Globalization brings people and communities of different cultural origins together in the same territory, and that is in process of turning everything upside down: both the old national political ideologies and certain basic social institutions.

The inadequacy of the economic and political attempts to get to grips with multicultural situations thus demonstrates the need also to consider the cultural and symbolic dimension of social functions. For no society exists outside a network of symbols structured by the imagination. Moreover the very idea of 'society' would disappear if the social dimension were not considered in a combination of its three basic authorities – politics, economics and cultural symbolism. In analyses these are customarily presented separately, but they cannot in fact be separated and are reflected each in the other, to give birth to what M. Mauss has called 'the complete social fact', i.e. the social as such, the essential moment when 'society or people become sentimentally aware of themselves and their situation towards others'.

To grasp the cultural and symbolic factors in globalization we might recall that in her reflections on the origins of totalitarianism, Hannah Arendt already saw the minorities, the refugees and the stateless as 'the most symptomatic group of contemporary politics'. Its paradox, she remarked, was that it corresponds most closely to the universal and abstract definition of human rights and yet is almost always deprived of real legal protection. Thus the absence of a recognition of real belonging for the tens of millions of individuals 'originating from elsewhere' will probably be one of the major social tensions that we have to live with over the next few decades.

As well as the problems of redeveloping identities which the new situation requires, one difficulty is that we can hardly look to the social forces which existed alongside the traditional trade unions and political parties to resolve this social tension. For these essentially became defenders of rights acquired and privileges already established within the existing framework of the states. That is why the problem that some people do not belong to society by virtue of birth or culture will increasingly be accompanied by the opposition of which the 'moral minorities' show themselves to be capable – by 'moral minorities', I mean groups of individuals who are determined not to lose their prime advantages and to press as hard as possible in public decisions to ensure that justice is done to the marginalized who are deprived of their rights.

The churches, which in principle have no economic and political interests to defend, should of course figure among the 'moral minorities' mentioned here. But is that really how they want to be understood? For in order to bring into being what could be called 'the effective history of the vision of the gospel in the world', their action clearly needs to go beyond the liturgical level internal to their own functioning, on which they can content themselves with staging symbols of love addressed to symbols of humanity. They may even need to go beyond the charitable level of giving aid to those who are victims of what are now composite societies. For the churches, that means that over and above the spiritual demands of their service to their members and the duties of material compassion which they recognize towards outsiders, they have the irreplaceable task of elucidating their possible intellectual and moral – and hence theological – involvement in the current inability of what are now multicultural societies to get groups of different origins living together in a coherent whole.

However, before touching on this last question we need to take a detour and put the ambivalent role of the cultural symbols that are produced – of which theology is one – in the context of the edification of human societies.

The ambivalence of the cultural and symbolic sphere

Here I take the notion of culture in its broadest anthropological sense, as the externalization of the conscience and the reflexivity of the social agent. This notion refers to E. Cassirer, who defines human beings as 'symbolic animals' rather than as uniquely rational beings. The symbols produced by the imagination and by rationality play a part in the social and cultural construction of reality, in that they constantly aim to put the world in a particular state, in the same way as economic or political practices, but in different forms. Human beings invent language which ensures communication with others; imagine symbols which confer meaning on the world and give it a horizon; place themselves in traditions which tell them where they come from and where they are going; set up institutions which give their life a form, a protection and a substance. These symbols must be seen in the framework of the activity by which a group of people is brought together through their thoughts, dreams, criticisms or aspirations. Thus they transform what was initially only a destiny imposed by fate into a choice which, while not perfectly rational, is nevertheless better thought out. In this sense culture is the prowess by which people distance themselves from nature and forge a world of their own.

However, culture can produce reactions and go beyond what was expected of it. It then turns against its authors, as something opposed to the world that they wanted to construct. Then traditions no longer indicate the direction to be taken but place obligations on people to venerate their heritage. Institutions come to be no more than monuments built on a foundation of servitude, which guarantee only an illusion of eternity through an authoritarian guidance of human movements. The rules are no more than the source of a constant surveillance which engenders an incessant fear of transgression and punishment. Value systems and ideologies restrain freedom of thought, and an 'objective culture' seizes bodies and spirits, to keep them in its power.

Moreover, on the basis of a common anthropological foundation, there is no longer just one culture, but cultures which cross or even oppose one another. That is why cultural symbols never cease to engender in their authors contradictory feelings of involvement with and dissociation from the figure of themselves which shows through the cultural worlds that are produced, or attitudes of either acquiescence in or critical denial of the social roles which are prescribed. Thus, because the sphere of cultural and symbolic activity does not share out unified messages, but rather multiple messages which are regularly incompatible, it cannot in any way be seen and accepted as the instrument of a unilateral integration of all from a single centre, which comprises the norms of the majority or the dominant element in society.

That means that the sphere of cultural activity is far from constituting an area of harmonious and peaceful practices. Rather, it is a field of 'disputed questions' which the individuals and groups mobilize as resources in their incessant quest of identification and hierarchical classification. The ambivalence of cultural symbols is such that in them are interwoven the intellectual and moral ideals of humanity and the symbolic violence to which the will to power of human groups resorts, often without too many scruples.

It is important to emphasize this non-idyllic aspect of cultural activity because those who fight for a better world are often blind to it. They want to see only a potential new world in the encounter of cultures. But the conditions in which globalization takes place explain why this does not come about peacefully. Beyond the good sentiments of a garrulous humanism which sees the encounter of cultures only as promises of mutual enrichment, the observation of reality shows rather that there is a hierarchy of different cultures which is brought about by the transplantation of populations. On the social scene the cultures are not equal, because they do not all have the same dignity or the same power. There are cultures which confer social power, and cultures which confine people in social subordination. So the field of cultural practices cannot be considered *a priori* as peaceful, and there is no more reason to expect a marvellous equilibrium in the balance of payments in this sphere than there is in the economic sphere.

The cultural sphere must thus be regarded as an essential but ambivalent component of the intensive work that has to be done in globalized society so that in the process of differentiation and the formation of a social hierarchy of individuals and groups each may succeed in negotiating the presence and belongings which devolves on them.

The responsibility of the churches and theology

But to what degree can one claim that the intellectual and moral – and thus theological – responsibility of the churches should be involved in this social process?

Here we must not neglect, first of all, the fact that for the most part down history the Christian churches have contributed historically towards shaping symbolically the terms of the theological and political problem of modern societies. The conceptual pair 'universalism-parti-cularism' is profoundly associated with this. Certainly, today these churches have lost the public position which they occupied towards the end of the *Ancien régime*. But they have done so – above all within Roman Catholicism – without at heart renouncing the political theology which legitimated them. Thus if the struggle between the Catholic Church and modern society has lost its violence, it would not seem to have changed radically in nature. Moreover this church continues to produce a religious symbolism which does not contradict the political philosophy of the modern West in its universalizing intellectual claims. Far from it.

Now in thinking of belonging within the public space of multicultural societies, the stumbling block of political philosophy remains, as we have seen, the aporia which the conceptual pair universalism – particularism seem to come up against. However, we may well ask whether what has been considered the crux of the insurmountable contradictions in social relationships that this aporia is thought to reveal is not more a logic of power which the presentation under the form of an aporia simply disguises. For this aporia only expresses a political fracture of our time to the degree that it is accepted without discussion that social relation-ships must be thought of within the normative framework of an ontology for which the categories of the universal and the particular are defined as quasi-'natural', to the point that they becoming unquestionable, deriving from a kind of pre-verbal atemporal faith which comes to programme human conduct.

Necessarily, the form that human action takes in the framework of such a theoretical or doctrinal approach locates the contradiction between the universal and the particular as a pre-historical difference, which can eternalize the contingency of certain social forms and replace freedom with determinism. Thus the establishment of the political philosophy of states and nations affected by globalization in a position of supposed self-evidence and even transcendental necessity makes it possible not to endanger the social order which at present governs their public space.

However, does not the present situation of millions of people who find themselves with no place in society explode the vain pretensions of such a reified political philosophy? Does it not show the need to go beyond the aporia in which the concepts of the universal and the particular end up once they are taken as being ordained to safeguard a supposedly metaphysical reference, common and general, though its benefits only apply to some?

So we can see the importance of what in the political world is called the crisis of representation. We can also glimpse the need to add depth to a democratic culture which is manifestly unfinished. Finally, there is an invitation here to reconsider the rules which can make room for differences when they must co-exist with an 'us'. What is important today is the unprecedented perspective of what P. Rosanvallon has called a 'politics of subjectivity', implying on the one hand a new way of speaking of the individual and particular groups and on the other a new understanding of universality within the political bond.

However, in the sphere of cultural symbolism will theology contribute its share to this task of producing representations which will help people to build their globalized society in a new way?

Will theology, venerating its own heritage, remain the prisoner of the dogmatic constructivism of scholastic culture, the eternal and universal values of which play down finitude and disparage real life by a symbolic violence that is merely the consequence of its prior orientation towards the transcendence of being? For the Roman Church to adopt such a position would mean that in order to safeguard at any price its capacity to think of God in the same terms as it has since the thirteenth century, it would put the idea of God, this product of human culture, in the grip of a conceptualization which gives no lead in getting out of the philosophical and political impasse of globalized and multicultural societies.

Now if theology abandoned the position which attributes the power of proof to words rather than life, in other terms making the demands of freedom for human beings which are present within its evangelical heritage its theme, it would come back down to earth and provide significant support in the actual workshop of humanity. This would help theology to get beyond what today is an obstacle to the cultural and symbolic discoveries which it needs to make.

The multiculturalism associated with globalization makes the issues in the societies which seek to be democratic more complex. But the democratic inspiration – first as a cultural principle and then as a political system – has succeeded in establishing itself only where in the end it has been accepted that there is no longer a homogeneous and universally evident conception of the world, and that if one fails to take account of this one would inevitably move towards a situation in which some impose on others. If the plurality of world-views or interests could be surmounted only by reason or any other generally accepted system of knowledge, democracy would clearly not be necessary, since there would be an instrument for reconciling different or even opposed points of view. So democracy is another metaphysic, to allow individuals and groups which recognize their differences to live together, safeguarding the legitimate content of this diversity or at least that element of it which cannot be got over without the use of force by some. Simply during this century totalitarian political regimes, revolutionary parties and . . . the churches have been considered to be the depositories of the definitive truth on humanity. It is through their obstinate resistance to the principle of the democratic freedom of the understanding that these groups have regularly given themselves the mission of having their inspired truth accepted by all at whatever cost.

Without doubt democratic culture does not have the clarity of truth that ancient theological and political symbolism was thought to possess. Here democratic culture can be said to be post-Christian to the degree not that it has dismissed the religious element from the social scene but that it dissociates the absolute from the world, though they will never be mutually structured in the same direct fashion as they were. Nevertheless the consequences of globalization are present, and they make the democratic principle more imperiously necessary than ever. Yet in a confrontation with the culture of modernity, which cannot be dismissed, theology is replacing this with another older one, which theologians would prefer because they have invented it.

But in the end, what credit would be gained today by a theology which continued to preen itself on the subject of the privileged relationships which it claimed to have with the truth? Once the Kantian criticism of metaphysics and dogmatic theology has been accepted, it is more important for it to ask itself questions again about the 'something' which in the gospel heritage can take modernity beyond its aporias. And one cannot see how this 'something' can be found anywhere than in the divine representation brought out by the kenotic Christ, who says of himself that he has come not to condemn but to save the lost. So it has nothing to propose other than to 'save' modernity, i.e. not to reject it but to contribute, with all people of good will, towards transforming it. Hence it is hard to see why theology should ask people to abandon democratic culture, that specific culture which is theirs, to support another mental universe which is ecclesiastically more convenient.

So from the perspective of the originality of its social and cultural stocktaking – and beyond something that had long been assumed but has now returned to the filed of the common patrimony of humanity – the question is what contribution Christian theology could bring other than this Jesus whose concern for others, 'to excess', inspires a way of living which definitively purges humanity of inadmissible divine figures. It is by starting from there that Christianity, here differing from the cultural symbols of natural religion and ancient metaphysics, succeeded in conferring an invincible transcendence on the idea of God, that product of human culture. And in its wake theology succeeded in giving human freedom its content and at the same time the power of the sacred. That is because God does not tolerate, as metaphysics does, people being maltreated in the name of truth, abstract reason, strategies of whatever kind, or what are called the 'laws of history'. Besides, it should be pointed out that there are no laws of history in Christianity. There are only, closely connected, the idea of an infinite God in his love of humankind and the duty, which is also infinite, for everyone to have compassion on the fate of others. This overturns the social classifications inspired by the conceptual categories of the universal and the particular, although that comes at a price. Along this line the disciples must not expect to be excused the same ultimate test that their master knew.

Translated by John Bowden

Transcending Frontiers or Invading Territories?
Reflections on the Activities of the World Bank

Gregory Baum

Is the globalization of the free-market economy a process that transcends frontiers and fosters the unification and pacification of humankind? Or is it an invasion by the centre of economic power into the less economically-developed regions of the world, producing destabilization and impoverishment of the masses? In this article I wish to show that the World Bank itself has begun to ask itself this question.

The World Bank's commitment to neo-liberal policies

The World Bank and the International Monetary Fund (IMF) were created by the Bretton Woods Agreement after World War II to monitor the world economy, lend money to poor countries in urgent need, and prevent financial collapse on a universal scale. The Bretton Woods institutions increasingly followed the neo-liberal economic ideology that free trade and minimal government interference were the best recipe for the creation of wealth, ultimately to the benefit to all. The market was seen here as the engine that moved history forward towards universal well-being. When in the early 1980s the British Prime Minister Margaret Thatcher and President Ronald Reagan of the USA implemented neo-liberal economic policy in their respective countries, the Bretton Woods institutions were confirmed in their neo-liberalism and pursued it with greater vigour. (In English these policies are often called 'neo-conservative, because in Britain and the US they were introduced by the leaders of conservative parties.)

The neo-liberal policies had devastating effects on many of the poor countries of the South. To promote free trade and allow the free run of the market forces, the World Bank and the IMF imposed upon these countries the so-called 'structural adjustment policies'. These countries were to get no further loans unless they 1. opened their borders to free trade and the entry of foreign corporations; 2. deregulated the national economy; 3. privatized publicly-owned enterprises; 4. reduced government spending by cutting social programmes and laying off government employees; and 5. replaced production for the use of the population by production for export. These policies increased hunger and misery in many countries. Instead of growing their own food and producing the goods they needed, people were obliged to produce for export, which increased their dependency on the centre of world power. In the eyes of the World Bank and the IMF, this bitter medicine was necessary to contain what they judged to be irresponsible governments, discipline what they thought were lazy populations, and convince them that in the long run the self-regulating market system was the wealth-creating engine of world development.

The World Bank imposed these policies without mercy. Neo-liberalism became the new orthodoxy. Replying to its critics, the World Bank insisted that 'there is no alternative'. Yet alternatives had been offered. A well-known example is the 1989 Report of the United Nations Economic Commission for Africa, entitled 'African Alternative Framework to Structural Adjustment Programmes for Socio-Economic Recovery and Transformation', which thanks to the pressure exerted by the World Bank was never implemented. John Mehevc has argued that the manner in which the World Bank presents and defends its structural adjustment policies parallels religious fundamentalism.[1] Susan George, in her book on the World Bank's secular empire, also develops the theme of the World Bank's economic fundamentalism.[2]

Structural adjustment policies, we note, have been increasingly applied in the industrialized countries of the North. What has taken place is a major shift in the distribution of power and wealth. There are signs that we are entering a new phase of human history. Central controlling power has moved to the international financial institutions and the transnational corporations, none of which are accountable to the public or to any supervisory agency. National governments have lost the capacity to promote the well-being of their people and protect them from transnational corporations that enter the country, destabilize the local economies, and then invest the profits made locally in other countries. Observers have asked themselves whether the Bretton Woods institutions were envisaged from the beginning as a new kind of world power ruling in favour of the American empire. What is certain is that in the industrialized countries, neo-liberalism, as policy and ideology, has widened the gap between the rich and the poor, produced a growing sector of chronic unemployment, and promoted a culture of competitive individualism devoid of social solidarity and self-restraint – a culture resisted only by minority movements of spirited people.

The World Bank's concern for global governance

Criticism of the World Bank climaxed in 1994, the fiftieth anniversary of its foundation. The non-governmental organizations working in and for the Third World had organized a major campaign critical of the World Bank under the slogan 'Fifty Years is Enough'. This campaign informed the public of the destructive, undemocratic and unaccountable policies adopted by the World Bank and called for fundamental reforms of this institution. The campaign received massive support. In fact, the leaders of the G7 countries put the reform of the World Bank on the agenda of their 1995 meeting in Halifax.

In 1994, under its new president James Wolfensohn, the World Bank decided to listen to these complaints, enter into dialogue with the neo-governmental organizations, and modify some of its policies. The World Bank cancelled its involvement in a controversial project, the Narmada Dam, in India; it admitted that in many countries debt was a serious problem and prepared measures to alleviate it; it strengthened its commitment to reduce poverty in the world and, most significantly, began to hold meetings with the non-governmental organizations. It admitted their presence at the 1995 World Bank/IMF assembly and created a joint World Bank/non-governmental organization committee to review the structural adjustment policies.

What the changes introduced by the World Bank mean is a controversial topic. Some commentators think that the World Bank has adopted a new orientation, more beneficial to Third World countries, while others argue that these changes are largely window-dressing and do not weaken the World Bank's commitment to structural adjustment programmes and the neo-liberal logic that stands behind them.

Today the World Bank is deeply committed to 'world governance'.[3] Governance, we note, is not the equivalent of government. Governance refers, rather, to the interaction of several factors, including government and markets, in creating and sustaining order and peace in society, especially under the conditions created by globalization and its social and cultural consequences. The governance-producing factors besides governments and markets are summed up in the concept of 'civil society'. Civil society includes professional associations, trade unions, religious institutions, schools and universities, non-profit organizations, citizens' movements, cultural centres and – especially in the Third World – non-governmental organizations.

The World Bank's new concern for global governance may not only be due to the protest movement prior to its fiftieth birthday. After all, the World Bank shares the fear of all well-informed citizens that the globalization of the economy, undermining subsistence economies, cultural cohesion and social integration in many Third World countries, is producing conditions of grinding misery and social chaos that could easily lead to violent explosions. Such explosions would cause great human suffering. They would also threaten investment and private property, inhibit the production and delivery of goods, and hence be detrimental to the expansion of the free market economy. For all these reasons, humanitarian and economic, the World Bank has decided to encourage and support good governance, i.e. the ordering and pacification of society under conditions of poverty and dislocation.

In the name of good governance the World Bank now actively intervenes in Third World countries on several levels: 1. It puts new emphasis on role of the state; 2. It seeks co-operation with and offers financial support for non-governmental and other organizations of civil society; and 3. It recognizes and encourages the role of religion, ethics and spirituality.

The role of the state

The World Development Report, *The State in a Changing World*, published by the World Bank in 1997 puts a new emphasis on the role of the state. The neo-liberal theory and practice endorsed by the World Bank had favoured minimal involvement of the state in society, non-intervention of the state in the economy, and curtailment of national sovereignty in favour of the untrammelled international market. Did the 1997 World Development Report on the role of the state in the promotion of good governance represent a change of mind on the part of the World Bank? Has the World Bank softened its neo-liberal orthodoxy? On this question commentators are not in agreement. Most of them remain highly suspicious. The lengthy document, *The World*

Bank and the State: A Recipe for Change, published by the British Bretton Woods Project, carefully argues that the World Bank has not substantially modified its position. Its World Development Report of 1997 does acknowledge that the state has a role to play in 'protecting the vulnerable' through social welfare programmes and that it is not enough for states 'merely to deliver growth', but that they also have an obligation 'to insure that the benefits of market-led growth are shared through investment in basic education and health'. Still, when comparing these general remarks with the detailed prescriptions of how to deal with concrete problems and issues, it appars that the general remarks carry very little weight. The main task of the state, it would appear, is to ensure that the structured adjustment programmes are implemented under conditions of public order and peace.

Support for non-governmental organizations

The World Bank's relationship to non-governmental organizations has changed dramatically. Representatives of non-governmental organizations are invited to attend the major World Bank conferences and a number of joint committees have been formed. The World Bank, pressured by non-governmental organizations and other social agencies, including the Christian churches, has decided to introduce a programme of debt relief for the countries most in need. Yet the conditions laid down in the heavily indebted poor countries programme are such that a good many non-governmental organizations are disappointed and argue that the World Bank lacks the political will to work for debt remission, even in extreme cases. Even the World Bank senior vice-president, Joseph Stiglitz, has publicly criticized the heavily indebted poor countries initiatives as misguided and failing to address the fundamental issues.[4] Yet progress is being made in the joint committees reviewing the impact of structural adjustment programmes in various countries. This promising initiative, called SAPRIN, relies on the support and cooperation of the World Bank's president, James Wolfensohn. The non-governmental organizations participating in SAPRIN retain an open mind about its outcome. Yet the fact remains that despite the World Bank's willingness to listen to its critics, it continues to impose the structural adjustment programmes on Third World countries.

Whereas prior to 1994, the non-governmental organizations working in and for the Third World were united in their criticism of the World Bank, they have now become deeply divided. They differ in their response to the World Bank's offers of financial support for various kinds of self-help projects in poor urban areas. Since at this time the public funds financing the non-governmental organizations are shrinking, the temptation to accept money from the World Bank is very great. But is this money given so that the non-governmental organizations work among the poor to assure good governance under the conditions created by the structural adjustment programmes? Does the World Bank want the non-governmental organizations to offer small-scale remedies for the large-scale misery produced by its own inflexible policies? Are the non-governmental organizations becoming instruments for making the globalization of the free market economy more workable? These are the questions that divide them. Non-governmental organizations committed to an alternative vision of society and its economy are willing to accept World Bank funding if they are able to retain their autonomy, i.e. if they remain free to make their projects serve the needs of the participants, rather than the interests of the World Bank, and free to network with other organizations committed to an alternative vision and thereby promote a global solidarity from below.

Religion and ethics

Good governance includes support for an ethical culture that promotes social well-being. Inwardness or spirituality has social consequences. The world religions form patterned communities that sustain people in difficult times, strengthen them in their communal efforts, and create close bonds of friendship, co-operation and mutual aid. For these reasons religious communities, as part of civil society, play an important role in providing good governance. It is not surprising that the World Bank, faithful to its new image after 1994, has revealed a special concern for ethics and religion. Associated with the World Bank is now the World Bank Spiritual Unfoldment Society under the direction of Richard Barrett. The World Bank has sponsored several international conferences on religion, spirituality and ethics in the hope that a better understanding of the aims of the World Bank will allow religious leaders and teachers of spirituality to make a more focussed contribution to humanity's well-being. One should add here that the World Bank and its neo-liberal policies had been severely criticized by the Christian churches, their ecclesiastical leaders as well as their justice-and-peace organizations. Now the World Bank wants to hear and learn from the wisdom and experience of the world religions.

In this article I wish to comment on two such international occasions, the 1995 Conference on Ethics and Spiritual Values held in Washington,

DC, focussed on sustainable development, and the 1998 Conference on World Faiths and Development held at Lambeth Palace in London, England, focussed on co-operation between religions and the World Bank.

At the opening of the 1995 Conference on Ethics and Spiritual Values, James Wolfensohn, the World Bank's president, gave a keynote address entitled New Partnerships. Here are some of his words:

> Development is not just a matter of looking at increases in gross domestic product per capita. In Africa I saw successful development in villages where people were pulling themselves out of deep poverty. Development is visible in people who, within the structure of their familial or tribal system, possess a sense of grandeur, a sense of optimism, a sense of hope; who talk with excitement in their eyes about their children's future. These people, living on next to nothing, feel a sense of progress that is more than economic. It encompasses recognition of roots and their spiritual and cultural values, which we (the World Bank) need to nurture and encourage. These values are what we should be developing . . . The World Bank's central mission is to meld economic assistance with spiritual, ethical and moral development.
>
> It is not easy to explain to most people why I (James Wolfensohn) would leave a successful business practice to come and try to make the world a better place . . . I came (here) because of a background that had, I believe, within my own Jewish religion some sense of ethical, spiritual and moral values that I have attempted to live by and that guide me.[5]

The Proceedings published by the World Bank give the names of the thirty-four men and women who were invited to address the topic. All the speakers agreed that ethics and spiritual values must be taken into account in formulating economic policy, especially related to sustainable development. Most of them lamented the indifference of economics to ethical considerations, but failed, with one exception, to articulate a critique of the World Bank's economic policies. Only Denis Goulet, a well-known critical development economist, said in plain language that the economic globalization promoted by the World Bank undermined local economies and dissolved traditional values and that therefore, under the conditions created by these neo-liberal policies, environmentally sustainable development was impossible.[6]

My impression is that the World Bank Conference on Ethics and Spiritual Values remained on the surface. As we just saw, it did not offer a critical analysis of the values and presuppositions implicit in the World Bank's economic policies. With the exception of Denis Goulet, the speakers did not relate their remarks to today's historical reality. The Conference, moreover, bracketed religion: there was no sustained reflection on the wisdom and the values of the world's great religious tradition.

The Conference on World Faith and Development was held at Lambeth Palace, London on 18-19 February 1998. It was hosted by George Carey, Archbishop of Canterbury, and James Wolfensohn, President of the World Bank. Participants were leaders from nine world religions, including the main traditions within these religions: Baha'i, Buddhist, Christian, Hindu, Jain, Jewish, Muslim, Sikh and Taoist.

The Conference at Lambeth Palace was preceded by a Round Table Conference on 'A Christian Response to the International Debt Crisis', organized on 16-17 May 1996 by the Anglican Community Office at the United Nations. This latter conference set forth the biblical and Christian foundations for ethical norms relevant to the economy. It assigned special significance to the Jubilee Year, mentioned in Leviticus, that demanded of the Israelites the remission of debts, the release of their slaves and the redistribution of land. The immediate purpose of the Round Table Conference was 'to express uncompromising concern with the human impact of IMF and World Bank policies' and 'to explore with the participants possible lines of practical action that might help alleviate the negative effects of (IFM and World Bank) policies on the poor and vulnerable'. The conference produced a series of policy measures which it urged the Bretton Woods institutions to take into account.[7]

One is allowed to presume that in response to the Round Table Conference, James Wolfensohn agreed to co-host with the Archbishop of Canterbury the 1998 Lambeth Palace Conference on World Faiths and Development. Here leaders of the world religions were engaged in sustained conversation with staff members of the World Bank. At the end of the conference, the two co-chairs made a joint statement summing up in eleven points the agreements that had been reached.[8]

Here is a brief summary of the eleven points:

1. The religious leaders and the leading staff of the World Bank are at one in their deep moral concern for the future of human well-being and dignity.

2. Human development must have regard to spiritual, ethical, environmental, cultural and social considerations.

3. Human well-being includes both rescue from suffering due to poverty and spiritual and cultural expansion.

4. It is important to listen to all the actors involved in development, including especially the local community.

5. The World Bank and the major religious communities agree on the need to continue the dialogue.

6. The religious communities will be allowed to influence the thinking of the World Bank.

7. Several joint working groups shall be established.

8. The World Bank staff wants more education regarding the world's religions, and the religious communities want more education regarding international development.

9. The religious communities have already contributed much to development projects: they will continue to do so with the backing of the World Bank.

10. A light and flexible steering group will monitor progress in this area.

11. Governments and international agencies are exhorted to join the search for better understanding between religion and development.

Is the ongoing conversation between the World Bank and the world religions good news? At this time there is no sign that the World Bank has qualified its neo-liberal dogma in its practice. Will the ongoing conversation open the World Bank to human aspects of development it had previously overlooked? Will the World Bank try harder to reduce world poverty and help in the conversation of a more just society? At the same time, we must ask whether this conversation will oblige the participating religious institutions, including the churches, to abstain from critizing the World Bank in public. Will these institutions play their part in supporting good governance under the condition produced by the structural adjustment programmes and thus making the world safe for neo-liberal capitalism and the accumulation of wealth at the centre of power?

We return here to the question posed at the beginning of this article. Does the globalization of deregulated capitalism promote the unification and pacification of humankind, or is it an aggressive expansion of economic empire to the detriment of the majority of the world's population? There are staff members of the World Bank who have begun to ask themselves this question.

Notes

1. John Mehevc, 'The Fundamentalist Theology of the World Bank', *The Ecumenist*, Vol. 1 (second series), July/August 1994, 74–80, and his book, *The Market Tells Them So: The World Bank and Economic Fundamentalism in Africa*, Penangi, Malesia 1995.

2. Susan George and Fabrizio Sabelli, *Faith and Credit: The World Bank's Secular Empire*, New York 1994, 96–111.

3. Good governance has been a great concern of the United Nations: see the UN Report on Global Governance, *Our Global Neighborhood*, New York 1995. Even prior to 1994, the World Bank had shown a certain interest in good governance: see George and Sabelli, *Faith and Credit* (n. 2), 142–61.

4. *The Debt Update*, Report and Analysis on Developing Country Debt, Issue 2, March 1998, 1.

5. *Ethics and Spiritual Values*, Environmentally Sustainable Development Proceedings, Series No. 12, The World Bank, Washington, DC 1996, 1.

6. Ibid., 9–11.

7. A thirteen-page statement of these recommendations plus the conference programme can be obtained from the Rt Revd James Ottley, Anglican Observer at the UN, 815 Second Avenue, New York, NY 10017, Internet: anglican.un.office@ecunet.org.

8. The documentation can be obtained from the Press Office, Lambeth Palace, London, England, SE1 7JU.

The Frontier of the Body and Social Frontiers

Jacques Audinet

I The body – a social link

Crossing a frontier is always a physical experience. The body is involved in it, through the cooking and the language, the gestures and the behaviour. For however great our good will, we never feel as much at ease in a foreign language as we do in our mother tongue. There will always be some little thing, the accent or a turn of phrase, which will betray our difference. And the charm of exotic cooking sometimes has unexpected effects. These first experiences are there to remind us that while crossing a frontier brings new discoveries and new countrysides, at the same time it reminds us of our physical limitations. Our bodies remind us all of our particularity. We find that we are circumscribed by the frontiers of our own body. We cannot do everything or speak all languages or explore all possibilities. Our bodies vigorously remind us that there is no humanity without differences, first of all geographical and physical differences. Enthusiasm for moving between cultures is tempered by the material possibilities and comes up against the ambiguity which characterizes every human enterprise in the time and space of the body.

The frontier of our bodies, like any frontier, both encloses us and opens us up. The body is the place in which, for each of us in our own particular way, a tangible social bond is constructed. Our bodies are where we encounter the other and at the same time discover our own identity; they are where we have exchanges with other human beings at the same time as we are imprisoned in an insurmountable solitude. Thus crossing a geographical or social frontier comes to reveal personal identity. It is 'elsewhere' that we discover ourselves, and it is by going abroad that we learn who we are. Hence it is between our own bodies and the social bond that the symbolic exchanges which govern our 'being in the world' take place. So it is not possible to set the individual's body – an impermeable monad closed in on itself and isolated from others – over against the group and society. The two interact at the same time, and the language of relationship to others borrows images, symbols, attitudes and prohibitions from the body. Thus the frontier of the body and the social frontier resonate with each other. The same codes, the same words, move from one sphere to the other, arousing the same wonder or translating the same fears.

1. The process of encounter

This process is taken to extremes in the case of an encounter with another land, when the social, political and cultural frontier reinforces the frontier of our own bodies. Then the differences are emphasized to the extreme. But why are they so often experienced as threatening?

How is it that such a process can have such negative connotations? For if the crossing of a frontier is a discovery of the other and oneself, at the same time encounter with a foreign land arouses fear and rejection. So how is it that after decades of teaching and education about the values of democracy the hydra of racism arises so easily in the developed countries, and talk of exclusion based on the rejection of others in their physical being, of the other as body, is again flourishing?

2. The vocabulary of the body

The vocabulary of social exclusion is in fact often a vocabulary which relates to the body. Alongside expressions relating to geographical space, there is a whole series of other expressions which only make sense when related to the body. Such a vocabulary is pejorative. For example: 'purity of blood', 'racial purity', 'ethnic cleansing', 'pure race', 'pure language', 'purely between us', and so on. In short, humanity is regarded as being separated into two groups by an invisible and subtle line: those who are pure and those who are impure. Such a schematization can be developed *ad infinitum*. For purity is marked by signs, and especially cleanliness. Strangers are said to be 'dirty', 'badly dressed', 'bad mannered', 'speaking badly'. And it is only one step from the physical to the moral: they are also 'lazy', 'badly educated', 'disorganized' and at the end of the day 'degenerate' and 'dangerous'. The presence of the stranger also brings a risk of contamination. The stranger's customs, denounced as dissolute, are 'contagious' and one must keep away from them. All these words, encountered in recent conversations, discovered by surveys or used in some newspapers, are the reflection of stereotypes which relate to primarily corporeal schemes which make transpositions from the individual body to the language of social relationships.

3. Purity of blood?

Each of these expressions has a history. Each has left its mark on the course of time and some continue to have devastating effects today. Their consequences are always present. One does not have to go back too far to find one or other of them being fully accepted and determining a policy. 'Purity of blood' represented an ideal for some people in sixteenth-century Spain at the end of the Reconquista. 'Purity of race' was one of the dominant elements in the Nazi ideology, and the sinister 'ethnic cleansing' continues to have its supporters in Europe and on other continents, at a cost of which we are all aware. But such stereotypes are far from being simple word-plays or superficial associations. They bring into play the codes of 'purity' and 'stain', 'health' and 'degeneration', and ultimately 'matter' and 'spirit'.

Purity, 'the quest for the absolute at the risk of humanity', according to the title of the journal *Autrement*,[1] represents the view of an unmixed identity. Very soon this makes its mark on the small child's body under the sign of purity. Purity/cleanliness is an acquisition which requires a long apprenticeship of the small human being. For children, this is the condition for mastering their own bodies, emerging from the confusion between themselves and objects, themselves and others, first of all their mother's bodies. So to exist is to be separate, to be capable of recognizing the frontier between one's own body and that of the other, emerging from a fear of fusion which is both fascinating and threatening at the same time. In this sense, to exist is to be oneself without mixture, to have integrity, to be pure. As Ricoeur notes: 'the fear of impurity . . . is focussed on the diminution of existence, the loss of the personal nucleus'. But in his view this is also a primitive fear, prior to the split of the ethical from the physical, and in a way has a 'pre-ethical' character. It is the work of the word to overcome this fear and to sublimate it.[2]

4. Ritual/spiritual purity

So it is not surprising that religions make purity an ideal. There is a ritual purity which separates the world of the gods from the world of human beings and traces the frontier between the sacred and the profane. There is a social purity which in some traditions is to be found as the basis of the hierarchy and of the organization of society itself. There is a spiritual purity presented as renewal of being, which is both psychological and relates to the identity. A whole education, at least in the West, banks on the sense of purity. This then becomes respect for the body, one's own and that of others. In Christianity, purity is the very condition of the validity of the relationship of love, of charity, which constitutes the bond of salvation to God and to others.

The old catechisms developed a teaching about purity which was both precise and radical. It was radical, because it left no alternative. There are no half-measures in purity, and the sins of impurity are considered serious precisely because to indicate the specific way in which one should act is to say what one should avoid. Such a virtue calls for the avoidance 'of everything that leads to impurity: thoughts, desires, looks, reading, words or actions'. The texts go into details here: 'the occasions which lead to impurity are: laziness, intemperance, dangerous friendships, dishonest conversations, etc.' So purity appears in modern catechisms no longer simply as that which sets the sacred world apart from the profane world. But it becomes a moral virtue which shapes the identity of the subject, requiring of it the most subtle actions, extending into the world of thoughts and intentions. The ambiguous effects of such teaching have often been denounced, but the benefit of the refinement of the conscience which it has produced has also been recognized.

II. Colonization and the language of the body

At the time of the expansion of Europe and colonization, skin colour was to become the indicator of purity in relation to the stranger. An arithmetic of colours became established from the sixteenth century onwards which distinguished between mulatto, quadroon, octoroon and so on, each word denoting supposed degrees of 'purity' of blood. Thus skin colour came to be likened to a stain. It became a criterion of superiority or inferiority. 'No one will question that the white race is superior to all others', wrote the *Grand Larousse* dictionary at the end of the nineteenth century. The white man is declared superior, and by virtue of that the others are inferior and bring danger. From then on we see the link between the words colour, race and power. Such a link was to govern the constitution of modern societies which emerged from colonization. The binary character of such a scheme should also be noted. Anyone who is not white is immediately disqualified as being 'coloured', and it is impossible for such a person to escape his or her condition.

1. Western thought and thought outside the West

The language current in the West continues to associate purity with whiteness. As François Madeiros has shown, colonization/civilization based on Christian preaching has rooted in people's minds the fantasy of purity.[3] Purity, light, spirit, whiteness are opposed to blackness, matter, obscurity, impurity. Both the sermons of the last century, for which the Indian and the Black are demons, and contemporary Europe, in which talk of purity of blood and the atrocious practice of ethnic cleansing is arising again, bear witness to the depth and permanence of these associations.

The secularization of our societies has not done away with the desire and the fears linked with purity. Perhaps today they present themselves in other guises. Hygiene and the fear of physical contact, smells and microbes can easily take the place of the obsessions with purity in ancient texts. But above all the fear of the alien remains tied to these infantile attitudes which are inextricably bound up with the desire for personalization and dissolution. Thus Julia Kristeva writes:

> Is it so certain that the 'political' feelings of xenophobia often do not include unconsciously this trance of jubilation which the English call uncanny and the Greeks simply *xenos*, 'alien'? In the fascinated rejection which the alien arouses in us there is a disturbing degree of strangeness in the sense of the depersonalization which Freud discovered and which links up with our desires and our infantile fears of the other, the other which comprises death, woman, the irresistible impulse. The alien is in us; we struggle against our own consciousness – this element of our impossible 'own' which is not our own.[4]

It seems to me that this rooting in the deepest levels of the psyche explains the radical and violent nature of the stereotypes linked with the alien. Racism ultimately finds its origins in the infantile fears linked with the integrity of the individual body. The other, simply by virtue of the fact of being other, different, is seen as being frightening. The other is the one who causes fear and threatens destruction. Hence the slightest difference arouses violence, whether this is skin colour or sexual difference. The strange woman then becomes that much more dangerous and that much more desirable. A relationship of desire/domination begins, built on violence, as witnessed by the monstrous practices of collective rapes brought about again by recent conflicts on different continents of the planet.

It is only a step from impurity to degeneration. Gobineau took it. For him, what characterizes human societies is the process of degeneration in which they are caught up.

> I think that the word degeneracy, when applied to a people, must signify and does signify that this people no longer has the intrinsic value which it formerly possessed, because it no longer has in its veins the same blood, since successive alliances have gradually modified its quality. In other words, although it bears the same name, it has not preserved the same race as its founders: finally, I think that the decadent man, the one who is called the degenerate man, is ethnically a different product from the heroes of the great eras.[5]

So the process of degeneration is bound up with purity of blood, of which human beings, and with them civilization, are a product. At the beginning of humankind there was a superior race which possessed 'the monopoly of beauty, intelligence and strength'. From it civilization arose. This was the white race, and all the great human civilizations have arisen on its initiative. The process of mestizaje or cross-breeding allows other civilizations to benefit from what is handed on by the white race, but for humanity it represents decadence.

For Gobineau, the biological element is what determines all human relations. For him, social differences are conceived in biological terms. In this perspective, what is attributed to the body is immediately transposed to the social bond: words like 'health', 'sickness', 'degeneration' become categories which claim to judge society and relations with others, with the binary character of such categories. Furthermore, biological differences are the foundation for social inequalities. In short, Gobineau claims to give a 'scientific' justification, to use his own term for pre-ethical perceptions of others. The code of health/degeneration reinforces that of pure and impure, tracing a frontier between oneself and the other, between the indigenous and the alien, between the 'civilized' and the 'savage', a frontier which cannot be crossed because it is grounded in 'nature'.

Tocqueville, who was engaged in correspondence with Gobineau, immediately denounced such a view: 'You are reducing everything to biology,' he wrote to him. To reduce the social and the cultural to the biological in this way opens up a way which is not only wrong but dangerous, since it dehumanizes the human being. Thus Lévi-Strauss notes:

> The original sin of anthropology consists in the confusion between the biological notion of race (supposing that even in a limited sphere this

notion could lay claim to objectivity, which modern genetics contests) and the sociological and psychological productions of human cultures. It is enough for Gobineau to have committed it to find himself imprisoned in the vicious circle which leads from an intellectual error which does not exclude good faith to the involuntary legitimation of all attempts at discrimination and oppression.[6]

2. The body of language and interpersonal relations

Gobineau's ideas are more than a century old. But no one could deny that they still form an undercurrent in our societies. Gobineau calls for bodily differentiations to be the basis for social differentiations, whereas for a society to survive it is necessarily for social distributions to deal humanely with physical differences. This is what democracies try to achieve with the concept of human rights and the recognition of the equality of all human beings. The relationship of the body to the social bond is constructed in the opposite way to that claimed by Gobineau. In it the body is not rejected as impure or the source of degeneracy, but finds its place as the place and language of interpersonal communication. This is a long struggle which is far from being over. Thus Vigarello notes:

> There is no doubt that the old Platonic tradition of the body as the 'prison of the soul' has lost all its legitimacy. In it the body was doubly rejected: by imprisoning the senses it obscured all certain knowledge, and by the attraction of pleasure it perverted every possible morality. Free thought was first of all rejected, in deliberate opposition to the body, a conquest imposed 'totally alone, by itself without mixture' so as the better to undertake the 'pursuit of each reality' (Phaedo). This made awareness the sovereign authority and the body a formidable obstacle: an obstacle on the way to the true, an obstacle on the way to the good. Christian tradition took up this division in its own way, making the body less an organism than a 'flesh' which any attempt at freedom has to overcome.[7]

To oppose the body to the spirit as the particular to the universal is to reinforce the schemes of 'pure' and 'impure', 'healthy' and 'degenerate', by an idealism which also in the end of the day denies the human. Binary categories betray the reality of humanity. From this perspective, then, intercultural relations, an exchange between human groups and a crossing of frontiers is not a uniquely 'spiritual' enterprise, an encounter with the stranger which forgets the differences. Inter-personal relations are not aseptic. Encounter with the other, the alien, does not only take place at a cultural level, understood solely as a work of the mind, leaving aside the other less ethereal aspects of the interhuman encounter. It is impossible to be 'colour blind'. Real humanity is a rainbow with a thousand nuances, and its model is neither the clarity supposed to be characteristic only of the spirit, nor what is claimed to be the capacity of the body, but, like the rainbow, the indefinite variety of combinations of colours.

On the contrary, the mestizaje which Gobineau deplores is the illustration and activity of the body in crossing frontiers. It emphasizes the arbitrary character of the separations made between human beings. It makes obsolete the claim to base social differentiations in nature. It rejects the social distributions built on the ideology of purity or blood. It brings to light the incoherence and hypocrisy of such views, since the child who is born comes from origins which social order opposes and wants to keep separate. The simple existence of the mestizo child makes any binary conception of the social bond obsolete. It puts in question the order which has been imposed and the symbolism which justifies it. It bears witness to the fact that those who impose the law are at the same time those who transgress it. By putting its finger on the hierarchy of unconscious values in a society, mestizaje brings out its incoherence and its violence. It reveals a social bond that goes beyond the frontiers.

III. Conclusion

Emphasis on this in a culture bears witness to a new attitude. 'Black is beautiful', and all colours are called on to unite, if only in advertising. Such an emphasis proclaims another way of establishing human brotherhood: no longer on an order which is claimed to be biological but on differences accepted in a properly human way, i.e. by law and contract for freedoms. Mestizaje in our multicultural societies is a permanent reminder of the unpredictability of the human adventure and the need for the democratic project. In this sense mestizaje is a paradigm of the intercultural. It opens up a way for humanity.

Translated by John Bowden

Notes

1. *La pureté, quête d'absolu au péril de l'humain, Autrement*, Série Morales 13, Paris 1993.

2. Paul Ricoeur, *Finitude et culpabilité II, La symbolique du mal*, Paris 1960, 33f.

3. François Madeiros, *L'Afrique et l'Occident*, Paris 1985.

4. Julia Kristeva, *Étrangers à nous mêmes*, Paris 1988, 283.

5. Comte de Gobineau, *Introduction a l'essai sur l'inégalite des races humaines*, reissued Paris 1983, ch.4.

6. Claude Lévi-Strauss, *Anthropologie structurale* II, Paris 1973, 378.

7. Vigarello, 'Découvert, pas toujours révélé', *Le Monde de l'Education*, June 1998.

Mestizaje:[1] The Birth of New Life

Virgil Elizondo

The star of France's world cup champions of 1998 was an Algerian Frenchman, the star of the USA golf tournaments is an African-Asian American (African American father and Thai mother). The new heart-throb of young women around the globe is a German-Italian American Hollywood actor. The President of Peru is a Japanese Latin American and Brazilian Japanese are dancing Zamba in the streets of Japan. At any major sports event, you can no longer identify the nationality of the players by their physical characteristics. In any small town or mega-city, the physical characteristics of the local people seem to indicate that a good part of the world is now living there. Business, the need for work, migrations and easy travel are turning the world into a small inter-connected village. Friendships, conjugal relations and marriages are breaking through old racial/national taboos and thus giving birth to a new humanity. Is this to be feared or celebrated?

I. Mestizaje: the ultimate transgression

Mestizaje is simply the mixture of human groups of different genetic make-up, determining the colour and shape of the eyes, skin pigmenta-tion and bone structure. The mestizo will thus be a person of undefined physical and cultural identity. It is the most common phenomenon in the evolution of the human species. Scientists state that there are few, if any, truly 'pure' human groups left in the world and that they are the weakest, because their genetic pool has been gradually drained. Through mixture, new human groups emerge and the genetic make-up is strengthened. Because the mixture is not just biological but equally cultural, it will be welcomed or abhorred, depending on the stereotype which the groups have of themselves and of others.

History clearly brings out that there is no difficulty with the physical mixing of peoples, but it is a completely different story when it comes to the social and cultural mixing of persons and of peoples. Biologically speaking, mestizaje appears to be quite easy and natural, but culturally it is usually feared, threatening and often even prohibited. It is as common as human history itself, and yet it is the great taboo of human history. Mestizaje is the bodily and spiritual transgression of the ultimate human taboo. It comes through the most intimate penetration of the most sacred space of the other – the sexual.

If mestizaje is such a natural thing, then why is it such a taboo? Just looking at the human story, we seem to have a built-in instinct to protect the boundaries of our existence as much as we have an instinct to transgress these boundaries through exploration and conquest – whether sexual, geographical, intellectual or otherwise. As human beings, we seem to have a natural fear of 'others' and of disturbing the unity of the group – whether family, clan or nation. This fear is so deep that the Bible and other cultures have found it necessary to prohibit marriages among immediate or close family members. The biological and cultural disturbance of the group's life, especially through intermarriage, is so feared that in many places it is still prohibited and in most others it is deeply frowned upon. Yet it happens! And it is happening more widely and rapidly than ever before.

In the eighteenth and nineteenth centuries, some added to this natural fear of mixture beyond one's group by promulgating the false ideas of the basic inequality of the races according to skin colour. Thus they saw any mixture with the so-called 'inferior' races as a degeneration of the human race. Even theologians sought to add biblical credence to these notions. This led to the justification of conquest and slavery, the sale of human beings, the prohibition of race mixture in the United States and to the destructive efforts to create a white master race.

Mestizaje is feared because it is the deepest threat to all the ordinary bonds of identity and belonging. It is a threat to the security of social belonging, that is, to the inherited national/cultural/biological identity which clearly and ultimately defines who I am to myself and to the world. It is an even deeper threat to established societies because the mestizo cannot be named with clarity and precision. So much is in the mystery of a name! I am comfortable when I can name you, for in many ways it indicates that I am somewhat in control of the situation. I may not like what I know, but at least I have the comfort of knowing what it is. But there is a nervousness when I do not know who you are – your name and your cultural nationality are so important, for they tell me who you are personally and fundamentally. They give me your immediate and ultimate human identity.

The mestizo cannot be named adequately by the categories of analysis of either group. He or she does not fit into the single history set of norms for testing and identifying persons. This is threatening to both parent groups – we mestizos can name them and even study them, but they cannot name us or even figure out how really to study us. We are the 'between' people, for our very existence includes portions of both while not being fully either! As such we can see and appreciate the aspects of both which neither see of themselves or each other. In this 'between' existence lies the potential for our creativity: to pool the cultural genes and the chromosomes of both so as to create a new one!

II. The trauma of birth

Mestizaje could certainly come in various ways, but it is a fact of history that massive mestizaje giving rise to a new people usually takes place through conquest and colonization or massive migrations. This has certainly been the case with the Mexican and the Mexican American mestizaje. The first one came through the Spanish conquest of Mexico beginning in 1519 and the second one started with the Anglo-American USA invasion of the Mexican North-West beginning in the 1830s and continues today through the migration of the US way of life into Mexico and of Mexicans into the United States. Massive migrations from the south to the north and from the east to the west are producing new mestizajes throughout the Western world. Mixture is taking place at every level of human life from the gastronomic to the erotic, and even to the spiritual.

In the ideal order, the exchange of genes and cultures would be mutually beneficial and enriching. However, in the real order of life, mesitzos usually suffer from the deep trauma of non-belonging, non-identity and often even shame and disgust at being who they are. From earliest childhood, they will struggle with the question 'Who am I?' The image of the conqueror-colonizer or of the dominant host culture as 'superior/beautiful' and of the conquered or immigrant as 'inferior/ugly' will be imposed and interiorized by all the media of communication: dress, food, manners, language, modes of thinking, art, music, bodily gestures, mannerisms, entertainment, and all the institutions of society, such as the family, economics, school system, politics and, most of all, by the religious imagery and mythology. This relationship is irreversible and can never be totally removed or abstracted from. The totalitarian image which colonizing Europe established and implanted in the colonized peoples as the universal model for everyone continues to have a determining influence around the world. This 'normative image' of Western civilization continues to be reinforced and projected through television and movies, books, periodicals, universities and the European-controlled religions. Only the white Western way appears as the truly human way of life, while all others continue to be related to an inferior status. This is not necessarily a conscious effort, but merely the ongoing and unquestioned arrogance of the West, as subconsciously it continues to see itself as the model and master of the world.

Yet, in spite of the difficult situation of inequality, the very seeds for the destruction of this dichotomy of 'superior/beautiful' versus 'inferior/ugly' are physically implanted through the process of mestizaje. Through bodily intercourse and intermarriage, a new biological-cultural race is born who will be both conqueror and conquered, immigrant and native, superior and inferior at one and the same time: he or she will be a real blood sister/brother of both, without being exclusively either.

The mestizo is born out of two histories, two cultures and two genetic pools, and in him/her begins a new history, a new culture and a new genetic being. The physical, symbolic and mental structures of both histories begin to intermingle so that out of the new story which begins through the mestizo's body, new meanings, myths and symbols will slowly and painfully emerge. They will be incomprehensible to people who try to understand them through the meanings, mythologies and symbols of either of the previous histories alone.

The deepest suffering of the mestizo comes from what we might call an 'unfinished' identity, or better an undefined one, which produces a deep sense of impurity, of not belonging to either of the parent groups. One of the core needs of human beings is the existential knowledge that regardless of who I am socially or morally, I AM. I belong; I am truly one of the group; this is my territory. The knowledge of fundamental belonging, that is, to be French, American, Mexican, English . . . is one of the deepest needs of persons. When this need is met, it is not even thought about as a need; but when it is missing, it is so confusing and painful that we find it difficult even to conceptualize it or to speak about it. We strive 'to be like', but we are not sure just which one we should be like. As Mexican Americans, we strive to find our belonging in Mexico or in the United States, only to discover that we are considered foreign by both. Our Spanish is too Anglicized for the Mexicans and our English is to Mexicanized for the Anglos.

In the case of Mexico, it was the mestizo image of our Lady of

Guadalupe which provided the beginning of the new social-cultural synthesis which would give meaning and identity to the mestizo bodies of the new-born European-Indian children. Her mestizo beauty surpassed that of all others. Our Lady of Guadalupe was not merely an apparition, but a perfect synthesis of the religious iconography of the Iberian peoples with that of the native Mexican people into one coherent image. It provides a common religious experience through which even the most diverse peoples can experience family unity and belonging. This marks the cultural-spiritual birth of the new people of America. Both the parents and the child now have one common symbol of ultimate being and belonging. For the first time, they can begin to say 'we are'.

III. The dynamics of new life:

The potential for newness will not be actualized automatically. The mestizo can simply strive to become like one of the parent groups, a goal which will never be achieved. However, mestizos can equally, although with more hidden difficulties than anyone suspects, choose to live out the radical meaning of their new being. This is exciting but difficult because, even though the dominant way may be rejected totally and explicitly, subconsciously the oppressed will strive to become like the oppressor, since they have already assimilated many of the characteristics of the dominant group. Will the group simply obtain power and acceptance by reverting to the ways of the parent group or will they initiate new life? That is the key question.

In the first stages of the struggle to belong, the first generations of mestizos will try desperately to become like the dominant group, for only they appear to be fully civilized and human. This will be especially difficult for the mestizo children and young people, for it will produce a tension between wanting to identify and belong to one of the parent groups while feeling they are betraying the other. They will even feel that there is something wrong with them, a sort of contamination! This is the result of the superior-inferior / beautiful-ugly image which has been projected and somewhat interiorized. This struggle includes every aspect of life, because the whole world structure of the dominant will have been assimilated and made normative for human existence. It equally involves a violent rejection and even a sense of shame at the way of the conquered or immigrant, because it appears to be inferior. The Latin American mestizo has been ashamed of an Amerindian background and tried to hide or forget it. Dark-skinned persons have tried to whiten their skins, and children of immigrants in the USA have successfully not-learned the language of their parents. Only the scholars of the dominant group will appear as credible, only their universities as prestigious, their wisdom as true, their language as civilized, their medical practices as scientific, and their religion as true religion.

Some of the marginated mestizos will make it into the world of the dominant society only to discover that they will never be allowed to belong fully and furthermore that down deep inside they are still somewhat 'other'. No matter how hard they have tried and how much they have succeeded, they still do not fully belong. This gives rise to a kind of schizophrenic existence.

This very pain of not being able to belong fully also marks the beginning of a new search. The ones who choose not to join the struggle to become like the dominant ones will tend to reject the world of the dominant in a total way: absolutely nothing good can come out of it. They will not only reject it but will hate and distrust it passionately. The only way to treat the dominant ones is to get rid of them or to isolate themselves from them. It seems that nothing good can come from them or their ways. This leads to constant frustration and even ethnic or religious wars of purification!

The period of the rejection of the dominant culture can also lead to a new beginning, to a recognition of the new life which is beginning to emerge. Even though biologically this new life begins from the very start, it will take time for the cultural identity to emerge as a distinct identity of its own. This new identity struggles to form its own unique individuality. It accepts from both parent cultures without seeking to be a replica of either. It is like the maturing child who no longer tries to be like the mother or like the father, nor simply to reject both of them, but is just himself or herself. Through the pains and frustrations of trying to be what we are not, the uniqueness of our own proper identity begins to emerge. It is an exciting moment of the process, and usually the most creative stage of the life of the group.

In the beginning, knowledge of ourselves will be a confused one, because we see ourselves through a type of double image, that is, through the eyes of the two parent groups. As the group develops, its own proper image will begin to emerge, and it will be easy to study ourselves more critically – not evaluating ourselves through the categories of either, but developing our own criteria of judgment and evaluation. As usual, it is the poets, the novelists, the artists, the comedians and the musicians who begin to paint, to sing and to suggest the new identity. Then the critical thinkers join in and begin to deepen, to conceptualize, to verbalize and to communicate the reality of our identity. The challenge is to blend our two traditions, our two historical processes, in a conscious and critical, creative way so as truly to produce a new body of knowledge and know-how, a new way of life for humanity, new values, new language, new criteria of judgment and acceptability. Yes, and even new expressions of religion, as antagonistic religions find a new common ground for the sake of humanity.

For me as a Christian, the mestizo is the biblical 'rejected stone which has become the cornerstone'. Mestizaje offers new break-throughs – initially they might appear as transgressions of even the most sacred, but in reality they are the beginnings of new life. We are bringing together in our body and soul what had previously been opposed. As Mexican Americans of the Southwest of the United States, we are the incarnation of Latin Europe, native America and Nordic Europe through Anglo-America (USA). Given the unique moment of history with its growing ethnic and wars of religious purification, we become conscious that our mestizaje can be a model for the new global family of the third millennium.

Our challenge is to discover, formulate and put into practice a new way for the production of a new culture and civilization that will neither merely copy nor blindly reject the cultures out of which we are emerging. We have to borrow creatively and synthesize from the best of all so as to introduce a more human world order. This will not happen automatically.

Old forms of being, identity and belonging are no longer adequate for today's humanity. The planet has become a small inter-connected village. Dividing each city into mini-nations is absurd. New paradigms are urgently needed if we are to survive together in peace and harmony. Wars of ethnic or religious purification will be more intensive and destructive of all. Old ethnic, religious and racial boundaries need to dissolve through the emergence of new life. Cultures will not die or disappear but simply continue through new flesh and spirit, in the new body and soul of the mestizo children. Indeed, the future is mestizo, new life where cultures meet!

Notes

1. In this article, I do not attempt to write about mestizaje in general but reflect on the reality of mestizaje from my own personal experience and that of my Latin American people. We are the product of the massive mestizaje initiated by the conquest of 1492 and continuing through migrations to our day. We are a biological, cultural, linguistic and religious combination of native America, Latin Europe, Africa and Anglo-Saxon America (which, of course, is the United States).

Disciplinary Boundaries: Rethinking Theories and Methods

Ananta Kumar Giri

What we are proposing is 'border crossing with a difference' – as an act of creation rather than one of violation. In methodological terms, remapping the borders between disciplines contributes to the larger intellectual project of rethinking culture, canon and disciplinarity.

Border crossing yields what W. E. B. Du Bois calls 'double vision' – it expands our field of vision without being expansionist; it includes without consuming; it appreciates without appropriating; and it seeks to temper politics with ethics.[1]

Disciplinary boundaries and the problems of modernity

Academic disciplines have exercised a dominant influence in the way we think, perceive and seek to understand reality and the universe in the modern world. Modern modes of inquiry into the human condition have been characterized by a disciplinary mode – it makes sense of the world through particular, specialized and bounded disciplines. We look at the world through the eyes of the discipline to which we belong and tend to think that the whole world is characterized by a disciplinary significance. If one is a sociologist, one tends firmly to believe that the world is sociological, while if one is a psychologist then the world presents itself to one only through psychological themes and figures – through the eyes of Sigmund Freud, as it were. Academic disciplines provide not only cultural frames to us but also social identities and locations in the institutions of knowledge. Academic disciplines help us to classify not only the world but also ourselves. And both of these functions and objectives are fulfilled by the erection of rigid boundaries among them.

But the rigidity of disciplinary boundaries in the seeking of knowledge has its genealogy in the discourse of modernity, the process of modernization and the formation of the nation state, the colonialism and the structuration of the modern university system. Modern disciplines work with an ideologically surcharged assumption that disciplinary boundaries reflect the different essences of different segments of reality. But what we are increasingly coming to realize now is that the boundaries between them are contrived ones and their specialization and monopoly over their disciplinary territory were part of a modern academic division of labour.[2] This is easy to understand when we examine the goals and striving of disciplines such as sociology and anthropology. There is nothing essential about the subject-matter of either of these two disciplines, as both deal with human beings and their socio-cultural worlds, but still their practitioners have built impenetrable fortresses around them. The royal subjects who live in these enclosed palaces have continued to live under the illusion that the subject-matter they so tightly cling to has been chosen by themselves. But if anthropology was to be the disciplinary and disciplined caretaker of the savage, then this 'savage' slot was not anthropology's own choosing, it was assigned to anthropology. In the discursive field of modernity the savage, the subject-matter of a discipline such as anthropology, made sense only along with a construction of an utopia, while 'utopia itself made sense only in terms of the absolute order against which it was projected, negatively or not.'[3] Thus in constituting an area of study around a thematic unit such as the savage, 'the internal tropes of anthropology matter much less than the larger discursive field within which anthropology operates and upon whose existence it is premised'.[4]

New movements of criticism and creativity

The above critical reflection on the genealogy of one's disciplinary object and the interrogation of the authority of one's discipline is part of a broader movement of criticism and creativity both within the academy and outside it which presents us with a picture of 'blurred genres',[5] where it is difficult not only to label authors but also to classify works in terms of disciplinary boundaries. For instance, how do we read the works of a scholar such as Michel Foucault or Jurgen Habermas? Here categorizing them with any single label such as philosopher or historian is not enough. In such works what we witness is not only the redrawing of maps of disciplines but also an 'alteration of the principles of mapping'.[6] Such alterations and transmutations have been made possible by the working of many scholars who find their individual disciplines inadequate and embody in their work a transdisciplinary conversation.

It is helpful, then, to listen to the perspectives and experiences of some creative experimenters who in their work have negotiated between different disciplines and in the process have created knowledge which stands at the alchemical meeting-point of several disciplines. Here we can start with the strivings of Amartya Sen, whose work embodies a creative transgression of many disciplinary boundaries – economics, sociology and moral philosophy, to name just a few. Sen believes that both economics and sociology deal with the 'complexities of social living' and tells us: 'I believe the task of integration of economics and sociology would be much easier if we recognized clearly how large an area of congruence we have. The immediate objects of attention are much more disparate than our respective ultimate concerns.'[7] Like Sen's, the Indian social scientist Andre Beteille's work provides us a much wider view of social reality which defies easy disciplinary classification. But after devoting a life-long career to conversations between sociology and anthropology, what Beteille writes challenges us to think far beyond: 'Sociology must surely remain receptive to the ideas of great anthropologists – Malinowski and Evans-Pritchard, and also Frazer and Lévi-Strauss – but I find it difficult to pretend that it has today any special relationship with anthropology that it does not have with history, economics or politics.'[8]

Transdisciplinary conversations and a new alchemy

Rajni Kothari is another of our contemporary transdisciplinary inter-locutors who, initially trained as a political scientist, embodies the interpenetration of many disciplinary perspectives and a dissatisfaction with the institutional and discursive boundaries of modernity which structure present-day academic disciplines. For Kothari, interdisciplin-ary research is not an end in itself and must be related to historical problematics – primarily the epochal challenges of multi-dimensional self and social transformation at present – and to alternative praxis.[9] Kothari argues that central to the process of transdisciplinary research is an alternative chemistry of knowledge-formation. This requires the forma-tion of an alternative community of seekers and a self who conceives of his or her role as primarily a seeker and a transformer. Kothari urges us to realize the limitations of the dominant framework of knowledge, i.e. the modernist framework of knowledge within which we pursue our inquiries and even border-crossing enterprises. For Kothari, the framework of modernity promotes a 'narrowly utilitarian view of science based on a conception of knowledge as an instrument of power in man's search for control and domination'. Such a modernist equation of knowledge and power gives rise to the deification of the professionals and technical experts in the human condition who systematically erase alternative traditions of thinking about knowledge, for instance, knowledge being concerned with understanding, love and selfless devotion to humanity. The modernist framework of knowledge alienates the man of knowledge from the wider social and cosmic reality and moves towards transdisciplinary formations. These have to be part of a broader effort of the struggle against modernity and a 'dialogue of civilizations, implicit in each of which is the notion of alternatives'.

Another recent effort which provides a similar broad agenda of transdisciplinary experimentation is the Report *Open the Social Sciences*, prepared by the sociologist Immanuel Wallerstein and his eight colleagues coming from various disciplines.[10] For Wallerstein et al., the urgent challenge for all disciplines now is to open themselves from their conventional rigidities and boundaries and break their chains of scientific and disciplinary illusions. Sciences should open themselves from their bondage to Newtonian mechanics, and social sciences should break away from their uncritical tutelage to the natural sciences. Developments in science, in realms such as quantum physics, point to the inseparability of the measurer from the object and process of measurement. Overcoming the modernist dualism of subject and object then seems to be an important step in the process of a needed opening up of our disciplinary and disciplined horizons. It is demystifying to read Wallerstein et al. write: 'If social science is an exercise in the search for universal knowledge, then the "other" cannot logically exist, for the "other" is part of "us" − the "us" that is studied, the us that is engaged in studying.'[11]

If Wallerstein et al. urge us to demystify modern science, then both C. T. Kurien and Herbert Simon in their inimitable ways urge us to demystify the cult of professionalism. Kurien tells us in his engaging *Rethinking Economics: Reflections based on the Study of the Indian Economy* that it is the cult of professionalism which makes economists safely reside in the artificial world of model building, oblivious of 'the links between the world of the professionals and the world which is the basis of their beings'.[12] And the Nobel-prize winning economist Herbert

Simon offers us the ideals of a pilgrim or a journeyman in place of the tight-necked professional and urges us to realize:

> Disciplines, like nations, are a necessary evil that enable human beings of bounded rationality to simplify the structure of their goals. But parochialism is everywhere, and the world sorely needs international and interdisciplinary travellers who will carry new knowledge from one cave to another.[13]

The challenge of transcendence

Acquaintance with the above experiments teaches us that transcending disciplinary boundaries requires the formation of new institutions for the pursuit of knowledge as well as the cultivation of a new mode of being. But institutional reconstruction in the agenda of transdisciplinarity is not confined to mere reconfiguration of the internal patterns of institutions such as creating new centres and new alliances within or outside the university system. It must question the socially alienating base and the modernist orientations of contemporary universities which seem to forget that there is an outside social world and promote specialized professionals who speak an 'arcane language' and are cut off from any wider public discourse. Thus institutional reconstruction and the striving of individual scholars have to be part of broader socio-political and spiritual movements.

One critical issue here has to do with the conceptualization of knowledge in terms of power. If knowledge is viewed as giving us power rather than a better preparedness to participate creatively in the dynamics of relationships in life, then there is an inherent tendency to project the boundaries of this guarantor of power and to rigidify them. So, in order to break down these boundaries we need a new way of conceptualizing, feeling and relating to the process of knowledge creation within us. This way has to go beyond a power perspective and cultivate what Felix Wilfred calls 'self-emptying or kenosis'.[14] What we need now is a new ethics of servanthood,[15] and it is easier for those men of knowledge who conceptualize their pursuits as those of a servant to break their disciplinary boundaries than those who think of themselves as masters. Spiritual traditions of the world provide us such a calling of life where we are urged to realize that knowledge is not for the acquisition of power but for serving the world with a spirit of *bhakti*, a spirit of devotion.

It is also helpful here to be clear about two meanings of transcendence.

First, transcendence does not mean cutting off the ground on which one stands but widening one's horizon, to be able to look to the sky, as it were. Our fear that transcendence means destroying the very holding ground is a product of a misreading of the process of transcendence, which is integrally linked to the process of immanence. Thus transdisciplinarity does not mean cutting ourselves off from our disciplinary bases, just as going beyond our mother's wombs does not mean sapping the continued ties with our mothers. But this integral link between transcendence and immanence should not make us timid in realizing that transcendence also involves a conscious striving to abandon one's initial starting point. The courage to abandon one's familiar and identity-giving discipline is also an integral part of the process of transcendence, and in coming to terms with it, we can gain resources/insights from both Heidegger and the Indian perspective of *vanaprastha*. Heidegger says that it is important for human beings to abandon their homes and be strangers to themselves and move in strange lands.[16] Academic disciplines provide wealth, prestige, power and acclaim for the practising professionals. But having gained all these through our respective disciplines, at a certain stage we have to abandon our assuring grounds in order to be able to discover the unexpected truths of reality in the borderland and wilderness, as it were.

The Heideggerian goal of moving in strange land is part of his wider commitment not to grant any essential boundary to Being and reality. Such a view of reality is now buttressed by developments in quantum physics[17] and contemporary interpretations of the Upanishadic agenda of transcendence and the Buddhist notion of *sunyata*. The Upanishads urge us to realize the simultaneous need for concept formation as well as their abandonment. Shankara emphasizes desuperimposition as an inevitable part of understanding reality and calls it *Adhyaropa-apavada*, which means 'advancing an argument and rescinding it at the end; one advances an argument in order to inspire and orient the listener, and one finally rescinds the argument'[18] in order to enable one to launch upon the quest for reality which defies determinate structuration and is essentially open-ended. Similarly, according to the Buddhist notion of *sunyata*, what characterizes reality is not an essential and determinate structure but a 'dynamic *sunyata*' the significance of which is not merely genealogical, i.e. reality has emerged out of the vacuum, but works as a permanent destabilizer of any stabilized form. *Sunyata* 'ruptures the bounds of Western-style conceptual metaphysics, assuming instead the role of an emblem of liberation'.[19] When we endow our disciplines with essential truths and rigidify the boundaries between them, *dynamic sunyata* as a mode of engagement has the courage and capacity to rupture these boundaries and make us seekers in a wonderland.

One important challenge in thinking about transdisciplinary research is the challenge of synthesis: how do we arrive at a synthesis of perspectives? This requires a dialogue between different – mutually competing – disciplinary perspectives. Transdisciplinary striving, then, is a process of dialogue where truth and synthesis emerge out of dialogue, rather than begin with it.

Notes

1. Mae G. Henderson, 'Introduction: Borders, Boundaries and Frame(works)', in ead. (ed.), *Borders, Boundaries, and Frames: Cultural Criticism and Cultural Studies*, New York 1995, 27.

2. Clifford Geertz, 'Towards an Ethnography of Modern Thought', in id., *Local Knowledge*, New York 1983.

3. Michel-Rolph Trouillot, 'Anthropology and the Savage Slot: The Poetics and Politics of Otherness', in Richard G. Fox (ed.), *Recapturing Anthropology: Working in the Present*, Santa Fe 1991, 30.

4. Ibid., 17.

5. Clifford Geertz, 'Blurred Genre: Refiguration of Social Thought', *American Scholar* 49, 1980, 165-79.

6. Ibid., 166.

7. Amartya Sen in conversation with Richard Swedberg, *Economics and Sociology. Redefining the Boundaries,* Princeton, 266.

8. André Beteille, 'Sociology and Anthropology: Their Relationship in One Person's Career', *Contributions to Indian Sociology*, NS 27.2, 304.

9. Rajni Jothari, 'Towards an Alternative Process of Knowledge', in id., *Rethinking Development*, Delhi 1988.

10. Immanuel Wallerstein et al., *Open the Social Sciences. Report of the Gulbenkian Commission,* Lisbon 1995.

11. Ibid., 64.

12. C. T. Kurien, *Rethinking Economics. Reflections Based on the Study of the Indian Economy*, New Delhi 1996, 11.

13. Herbert Simon, 'Living in Interdisciplinary Space,' in *Eminent Economists: Their Life Philosophies*, Cambridge 1992, 269.

14. Felix Wilfred, *Leave the Temple: Indian Paths to Human Liberation*, Trichy 1996.

15. Ananta Kumar Giri, 'The Calling of an Ethics of Servanthood', *Journal of the Indian Council of Philosophical Research* XVI.1, 1998.

16. Fred Dallmayr, *The Other Heidegger*, Ithaca, NY 1993.

17. Donah Zohar and Ian Marshall, *Quantum Society: Mind, Physics and the New Social Vision*, London 1995.

18. Ramakrishna Puligandla, 'The Central Upanishadic Insights and Their Significance to Deconstruction and Theory of Everything', A Memorial Lecture delivered at the University of Madras, 1996.

19. Fred Dallmayr, 'Sunyata East and West: Emptiness and Global Democracy', in id., *Beyond Orientalism: Essays on Cross-Cultural Encounter*, Albany, NY 1996, 177.

II · Theological Reflections

A Dissident of Stature. The Jesus of Mark 3.20–35

Bas Van Iersel

Most rules are laid down to protect and to maintain the existing order. Moreover anyone who is not authorized to change the rules cannot change the existing order without infringing the existing rules and crossing frontiers. So frontier violations by one or more dissidents are more or less necessary for any change which is not introduced from above.

We are used to the image of a Jesus who transgressed the rules. We think in particular of rules like the sabbath law interpreted in a restrictive way (Mark 1.21–31; 3.1–6) and the rules for purity (1.40–45; 2.15–17; 5.41–42; 7.1–13), and of the conflicts in which these infringements of the existing rules resulted.

By contrast, we are less familiar with the notion that Jesus also crossed certain frontiers which are nowhere explicitly described, but nevertheless touch a much deeper level of the social forms of the society in which he was born and brought up, the Jewish Palestine of his day. Why are we not more familiar with this form of dissidence? Because we are not sufficiently used to connecting what we know about the tacit rules of this society with Jesus.

Sociologists have taught us that the people in the Palestine of Jesus' day, like those throughout the area of the Mediterranean Sea, were in part governed by different values and norms from those which hold for the present-day inhabitants of northern Europe and North America. Alongside other determining factors, these are above all their image of human beings, the importance attached in this framework to shame and honour, and the extremely important role played – not just in this connection – by the bonds within the immediate family.[1] Mark 3.20–35 certainly calls for discussion against this background. Because it is impossible within the space of a short article to introduce the parallel passages from the other Gospels, I shall have to limit myself here to the context of Mark itself. For the sake of clarity, I would also emphasize that in this article I am not speaking about the reality of the Jesus of flesh and blood but about the image that Mark evokes of him, which the well-chosen title of a book defines with the term 'the narrative Jesus'.[2]

Shame and honour

In Palestinian society in Jesus' day – as often even now in the area of the Mediterranean, relationships within society were governed more than they are in northern Europe and North America today by feelings of shame and honour. There were many aspects to this. First, the status attributed to people was governed to a greater degree than we are accustomed by the way in which others regarded them. Secondly, people judged others by what they saw and perceived of them. That applied not only to what others did but also to external factors like the area from which they came and the family to which they belonged. 'Who do men say that I am?' and 'Who do you say that I am?' (Mark 8.27–29) did not have the same resonance that they have for us. Of course people tried not to lose face but to save it, to avoid shame and gain honour. The value attached to this will not have been very different from that already expressed in the book of Job. On many pages of this book Job's sense of shame is illuminated. One of these passages is 19.13–19, where Job complains that he has lost face, that he no longer exists for his brothers and sisters, neighbours and acquaintances, former guests and slave girls; that his servant no longer reacts when he calls him, that his wife thinks that his breath smells and his sons think that he stinks; in short that everyone, including his friends and those who loved him, looks down on him or no longer notices that he is there. In other passages, e.g. 29.2–25, he describes how previously he was respected by everyone as a skilled speaker in the gate, how he was recognized as a deliverer of the poor, a treasured helper and benefactor of widows and orphans, of the blind and the lame, and as a sought-after comforter of those who mourned. Power and beauty, might and riches, wisdom and eloquence were to a person's honour; weakness and ugliness, dependence and poverty were regarded as shame.

Family ties

Accordingly, family ties played a greater role than they do now in our part of the world. First of all everyone felt most embedded and protected in the circle of his or her own immediate kin. As result families came to stand over against one another rather than to stand by one another. The culture of honour and shame of which a short summary has just been given also plays a part in dealings between families. Another point is connected with the relationship between men and women. The men are the defenders of the family and the women those who look after it. That means that the activities of the man take place outside the house and those of the woman within it. One thinks of Simon and Andrew who fish in the sea (Mark 1.16), and of Simon's mother-in-law, who at first lies sick at home but after being healed serves the guests (1.29–31). Because the father is out of the house, neither the girls nor the boys see much of their father while they are still children, and are brought up completely by their mother in the women's quarters. As a result boys have too few possibilities of developing their sexual identity and their male role from experiences with their father. This, too, leads to an exaggerated bond with their mothers and all its consequences.

Jesus and blood relations

Although Jesus' blood relations are not named in Mark before chapter 3, it is a mistake to think that the relationship is not mentioned earlier. That is implicitly the case the moment that Jesus appears on the scene. In 1.9 it is said laconically that Jesus leaves the Galilean village of Nazareth and has himself baptized in the Jordan by John. Was he at that time still a young man out for adventure? The story does not say so. What it does say is that in contrast to the people of Judaea and Jerusalem who came in crowds, he came alone; indeed he was the only Galilean to come to John. That is emphasized by the report that when he had received baptism from John he spent forty days alone in the solitude of the wilderness. There he had no other company than that of wild beasts and strange (heavenly?) messengers who looked after him.

Is he already showing himself to be a dissident here?

The impression that he has deliberately detached himself from his nearest blood relations in any case is already clearly confirmed in 3.20–22. After appointing twelve kindred spirits as helpers (3.13–19), Jesus has gone back to his house. That is certainly not in Nazareth, but presumably at a sort of *pied à terre* that he found in Capernaum (2.1; 7.17; 9.33). The members of his family have to leave their house to come to meet him. They think that he is out of his mind and with his deviant behaviour is bringing shame not only on himself but also on his family. Does Jesus know that? The story does not mention it either. But in 3.23–29 the

narrator puts words into Jesus' mouth which really assume it. At any rate
the story makes a close connection between Jesus' blood relations who
have come from Nazareth and the scribes who come from Jerusalem with
the accusation that he is possessed and drives out the demons because he
is himself an instrument of the chief demon. This suggests an alliance
between the members of his family and his deadly enemies (3.6). In the
middle of Jesus' reaction to these enemies we read: 'If a house is divided
against itself, that house will not be able to stand.' That is a general
statement, but at this point it can hardly refer to anything other than the
way in which the members of the family who lived with Jesus in Nazareth
under one roof are trying in one way or another to bring him back into
the fold.

How things will turn out remains uncertain until at the end of the
chapter the relatives come to the place where at that moment Jesus is
engaged in his activities (3.31). Only now does the narrator specify which
of the relatives have come to seize Jesus: his mother and his brothers.
That his mother is there is striking. As we have seen, women belong in
the home and leave what goes on outside to the men. But Jesus' mother
has come too. It is striking that when they arrive, the mother and the
brothers remain outside. We are not told precisely what this 'outside'
means. If Jesus is addressing people inside, it can mean the open air. If
Jesus is addressing people in the open air, then 'outside' is a place outside
a closed circle or a group of hearers which has gathered. For it is said
quite clearly here that a gulf has opened up between the members of the
family and Jesus. This is indeed so great that the mother and brothers
cannot speak directly to Jesus and have to be content with a message.
Either this is passed on from outside the house to the inner circle, or
someone makes their way to Jesus through the crowd.

A new family of spiritual kindred

The clarity of Jesus' reaction leaves nothing to be desired. First he asks
'Who are my mother and my brothers?' (3.33). Then, looking round at
the people surrounding him he says: 'These are my mother and my
brothers' (3.34). He then generalizes this: 'For whoever does the will of
God, he is my brother, sister and mother' (3.35).

If the movement hitherto can be described as one of Jesus breaking out
of the limits imposed by honour and family interest – and in that
framework as disowning his blood relations –, in the second half of the
episode, as readers we witness the formation of a new family. The blood
kin are replaced by spiritual kin.

There is a clear evaluation here. The verdict on the blood relations is explicitly unfavourable and negative. That is already evident to some degree from the rhetorical question in v.21, quoted above. But how negative the evaluation is is emphasized above all in the discussion in 3.23–29, that has been already mentioned above.

In the picture of Jesus presented by Mark we encounter the crossing of two frontiers. The first lies in the realm of family ties. Jesus leaves house and home, and that is far more than the protection of a roof. It is also and above all a whole circle of people who ask for care and attention, make demands and impose limitations. That here special mention is made of the mother makes it all the more pointed. The crossing of the second frontier relates to the honour of the family. Instead of honouring his family, in the eyes of his kinsfolk Jesus puts it to shame to such a degree that members of his family try to seize him to put an end to the shame. Instead of collaborating, Jesus widens the gulf with his family, rejects them and devotes his attention to a new family. On the one side he is a dissident and on the other he creates a new bond.

Jews and Gentiles

But these are not the only frontiers that Jesus crosses. Another and perhaps more important frontier that he goes beyond is the wider frontier of his village and region. Initially Jesus does not cross the frontiers of Galilee, but he does so in 5.1–20. However, this is not – as one might expect – to go from the villages in Galilee to Judaea and to the capital Jerusalem. No, the movement is in the opposite direction, still further from the centre and even the land. So it is a crossing of the frontier in the most literal sense of the word when in 4.35–5.1 Jesus goes over to the land of the Gerasenes. That is non-Jewish territory, as emerges from the fact that people keep pigs there (5.11). The way in which the crossing of the lake is described in 4.35–41 makes it clear that Jesus is portrayed by the narrator as the counterpart of Jonah. Jonah took flight on a ship because he rejected the charge to go to preach repentance to Nineveh (Jonah 1.1–3); while he was sleeping, the ship threatened to sink in a storm and was only saved when the crew threw the recalcitrant prophet overboard (1.4–15). After a journey in the belly of a giant fish Jonah was finally spewed up on a beach near Nineveh, arriving there against his will (2.1–11). By contrast, Jesus goes to the land of the Gentiles on his own initiative (Mark 4.35), brings deliverance from the storm by himself commanding it to be still (4.39), conquers a whole legion of demons in the Gentile country of Gerasa (5.1–15), and commands the person whom he rescues to proclaim the good news of 'what the Lord has done' in the Decapolis (5.19–20).

That in Mark the excursion to the land of the Gentiles is not out of place is evident when Mark tells in 7.24 how Jesus goes to Tyre and there frees the little daughter of a Syrophoenician woman from the grip of a demon, after the mother's urgent requests (7.30). In a previous discussion between Jesus and the woman, whom he initially does not want to have what she wants, the crossing of the frontier even becomes the central theme: if the children (of Israel) may be fed with bread, the dogs in the land of the Gentiles may benefit from the crumbs which fall from the table. Non-Jews were called 'Gentile dogs'. But now the taunt 'dogs under the table' has become almost a term of endearment. As I have already indicated elsewhere,[3] this story stands precisely between two episodes about a mass feeding (6.34–44 and 8.1–10). It is no coincidence that on the second occasion a number of those who take part 'had come from afar'.[4] That is already a technical term to denote Gentiles. And it does not seem improbable that the second story serves to make it clear that Mark's Jesus also reserves a place for Gentiles at his table. How positive his thought about the Gentile Romans is emerges not only from the passages already mentioned but also from the completely unambiguous way in which he puts on the lips of the Roman centurion under the cross of the murdered Jesus the words, 'Truly this man was a son of God' (15.39).

Structural

The frontier crossings in Mark that I have mentioned are not limited to the appearance of Jesus himself. On the contrary, they form a paradigm to which those who continue his activities must conform. It is within this framework that people who continue what he has begun (1.16–20; 3.13–15; 6.7–12) must clearly fulfil the same conditions as applied to Jesus. This is expressed – though less explicitly than in Matthew and Luke (Matt. 10.35–37; Luke 14.26) – in three passages: in the two ultra-short stories of callings (1.16–20), and in the passage in which Jesus' followers ask him what they must expect in return for all that they have left behind (10.28–30). It emerges from this that for him they have given up both their family ties and their means of support and their possessions; so they are following in Jesus' footsteps in two ways.

The crossing of the frontier between the Jewish and the Gentile worlds also returns – albeit in quite subtle way – where the story mentions the future of the disciples. That is the case in 13.9–10. There Jesus proclaims to them that they will be scourged in synagogues, but over and above that will have to testify to the cause of Jesus before governors and kings. The mention of governors and kings is already a reference to the non-Jewish part of the world, but the story adds that the gospel must be preached to all nations.

Consequently the ways in which Jesus crosses frontiers are structural and constitutive in the first formative phase of the Jesus movement.

Men and women

Finally, in another framework the crossing of a last frontier can be seen on the last page of the book. Up till then women were present on some occasions in the book as sick people to be healed by Jesus (1.29–31; 5.21–47; 7.24–30), and once Jesus praised a woman in an exceptional way because she had anointed him (14.9). However, important though these may be, they seem more like detached incidents. Only when Jesus hangs murdered on the cross does the reader unexpectedly get new and surprising information of a more structural kind: 'There were also women looking on from afar, among whom were Mary Magdalene, and Mary the mother of James the younger and of Joses, and Salome, who, when he was in Galilee, followed him, and ministered to him, and also many other women who came up with him to Jerusalem' (15.40–41). It emerges from this that – in contrast to what had previously seemed to be the case – Jesus had also moved women to go with him. The text explicitly says that here the women did not give up their role of caring. From that perspective, we may have here the hundredfold mothers whom in 10.30 Jesus promised to his followers who had left everything to follow him. But that does not alter the fact that they too had left house and home and like the men had become active outside the house. That was the case not only in his own territory, Galilee, but also on the road to Jerusalem and in Jerusalem itself. And it is important to note that here they not only make up part of the new family of the spiritual kin of Jesus but also part of the much more intimate circle of those who followed Jesus. Finally, in 16.7, they are charged to function as messengers of Jesus' resurrection.

The crossing of this last-mentioned frontier is certainly of no less significance than the two others, and also stamps Jesus as a dissident of stature.

Translated by John Bowden

Notes

1. See especially Bruce J. Malina, *The Social World of Jesus and the Gospels*, London and New York 1996. At many points this book raises two questions for me. The first is whether Malina does not identify the situation in the area of the Mediterranean today too easily with that in the first century. The second is whether he does not exaggerate somewhat when he suggests that something is specific to this part of the world. For the mechanism of honour and shame see also J. Pedersen, *Israel. Its Life and Culture*, Copenhagen 1926, 213–44. For the family see ibid., 46–96; C. J. H. Wright, 'Family', in *The Anchor Bible Dictionary*, New York 1992, II, 761–9; for the family ties in Mark see S. C. Parton, *Discipleship and Family Ties in Mark and Matthew*, SNTS Monograph Series 80, Cambridge 1994, 1–124.

2. O. Davidsen, *The Narrative Jesus. A Semiotic Reading of Mark's Gospel*, Aarhus 1992.

3. B. van Iersel, 'Die wunderbare Speisung und das Abendmahl in der Synoptischen Tradition', *Novum Testamentum* 7, 1964–65, 188–90.

4. Cf. Acts 2.39; 22.21; Eph. 2.11–13.

Jesus and the Syrophoenician Woman: A Tale from the Margins

(Mark 7.24–30)[1]

Dolores Aleixandre

My name is Eunice, which in Greek means 'good victory', though this is not what I was first called. My mother started calling me that many years ago, when I was still a child and lived with her, a widow already, in Tyre, the Syrophoenician city in which she was born, and so was I, over forty years ago now, and where I grew up. Now I live in Antioch, and when I hear my husband, Jonathan, go on so much about that city, I can't help smiling to myself when I compare it to Tyre, princess of ports and 'heart of the seas . . .',[2] 'the bestower of crowns, whose merchants were princes, whose traders were the honoured of the earth'.[3]

Jonathan, though he hopes I won't notice, can never get Moses' words about the Canaanites out of his memory: 'When the Lord your God brings you into the land that you are about to enter and occupy, and he clears away many nations before you – the Hittites, the Girgashites, the Amorites, the Canaanites, the Perizzites, the Hivites and the Jebusites, seven nations mightier and more numerous than you – and when the Lord your God gives them over to you and you defeat them, then you must utterly destroy them. Make no covenant with them and show them no mercy.'[4]

Nevertheless, the fact that I was a pagan didn't stop him from asking me to marry him. We met one day when the master of the house in which I was serving, a trader in purple like him, invited him to dinner to celebrate a good deal they had just made with another merchant from Cyprus. I remember that while I was waiting at table I heard him say that although he was born a Jew, he had embraced Christianity. He added that he owed his faith in Jesus the Messiah to some wandering preachers who came to Antioch when the followers of the Way began to be persecuted in Jerusalem.[5]

While I was serving him wine, he must have noticed that my hand trembled when I heard him talk about Jesus, because I realized that for the rest of the meal he was stealing secret glances at me. The next day he waited for me in the market place and came up to me as though he had always known me. He asked me if I had heard about Jesus, but that day I just told him baldly that I had been ill when I was little and had been cured thanks to him. I didn't feel able to tell him the whole truth yet, and he, though he perhaps felt that I was hiding something, didn't press me any further.

Before we married, he suggested that I should be baptized, and so I was, at the Easter vigil, surrounded by members of the community at Antioch, to which he belonged.

I soon realized that in that community there were two groups with marked differences: one of the Jews who had spent some time outside Palestine, who were much more open and tolerant (my husband was one of these), and another, less numerous but very influential, of those who had recently come to Antioch, having been baptized in Jerusalem, who were tremendously reluctant to sit down at table with converted pagans. They were scandalized by the fact that we had not belonged to the temple and the law, which were still charged with meaning for them; they did not hide their sympathy for James and were visibly reticent about Paul's decision not to impose circumcision because this, they said, undermined Jewish identity at its roots.[6]

Jonathan made benevolent excuses for them, perhaps because he too had come from Pharisee circles, although he had long been removed from the polemic that, years back, had made Jerusalem into a cauldron of conflicts.[7]

One day, during the meeting for the breaking of the Bread, one of them asked me if I recited the *Shema* morning and evening. When I said I didn't, he muttered under his breath about how right the Jews were not to accept those of my race as proselytes. My husband rallied to my defence and observed that some scribes admitted that Rahab the Canaanite had been an exception, but this annoyed them even more and they quoted Isaiah:

At the end of seventy years, it will happen to Tyre as in the song about the prostitute:
Take a harp,
    go about the city,
    you forgotten prostitute!
Make sweet melody,
    sing many songs
    that you may be remembered.[8]

The situation was so tense that one of the more moderate members of the community had to mediate, reminding them that Peter had welcomed the envoys of the centurion Cornelius and had then stayed with Cornelius in his very house. And that he had even said: 'You yourselves know that it is unlawful for a Jew to associate with or to visit a Gentile; but God has shown me that I should not call anyone profane or unclean.'9

They weren't convinced and even hardened their outlook still more; before we went our separate ways one of them – who never came back to the community – said to my husband, as a joke: 'Well, Jonathan, if I were you I should teach that Canaanite who lives with you what Leviticus says about the uncleanness of women.' Just that word 'uncleanness'10 shook me, because I wondered if he had sensed the condition I was trying so carefully to hide. I knew that the Jews, speaking of people possessed by demons, used to say: 'He is possessed by an *unclean* spirit,' pouring all their contempt on to that word, which for them meant a state of indignity, impurity and degradation such as we find difficult to comprehend.

I went back to our house distraught; it was a long time before I joined in with the community again, and then it was only my husband's patient insistence that persuaded me. The day I went back, we had a visit from Mark, a relative of Barnabas and companion of Peter and Paul on one or other of their journeys. We all knew of his sympathy for Christians of Gentile origin, and he was said to be putting together a collection of Jesus' deeds and words. One of the group of Judaizers started telling – obviously in order to show what he thought of Gentiles – how Rabbi Aqiba had named his two dogs Rufus and Rufina, and also how Rabbi Eliezer used to say: 'Those who eat with idolaters are like those who eat with dogs.'11

The mention of dogs dragged me back with the force of a furious wind to what my mother had told me so often and I had never dared repeat, and I realized that I had to overcome my fear once and for all. I took the word and, to everyone's surprise, used as they were to my habitual silence, I addressed Mark: 'If you are going to write about Jesus, let me tell you something you might like to know about him: when I was little, I was possessed by a demon, and although my memories are very confused, my mother often told me of the terrible times she had to stand by helpless and terrified while my body was shaken by violent convulsions and soaked in sweat, while I groaned horrendously and foamed at the mouth. She would hold my hand and stay by my side, caught in a storm of anguish and terror, until the spasms subsided and I came to myself with no recollection of what had happened and so pale that it looked as though the life had gone out of me for ever.

It was after one of these crises that she heard that a certain Jesus, whose healing powers everyone was talking about, had crossed the frontier separating Phoenicia from Galilee. So she decided to go and find him to ask him to cast my demon out from me. "And as I succeeded," she would tell me with a smile, "I gave you the name Eunice," and then she would go on to tell me the story I never tired of hearing: "He was in a house on the outskirts of Tyre and apparently trying to go unnoticed. I hesitated a lot before crossing the threshold, because I was afraid I might annoy him and that this would be counted against me, but you were sick, my daughter, and that gave me the courage to try to overcome any obstacle. I instinctively threw myself at his feet, but being careful not to brush against him, knowing the repugnance Jews feel toward us, and I said to him between sobs, 'My little daughter has a demon; I implore you to cast it out from her.' I didn't dare raise my eyes to his face as I heard him say what I had basically feared he would: that bread is for children and they have to eat their fill at the table before it is thrown to the house-dogs under it. In despair, I thought my words had shattered against the impenetrable wall built between that Jew and me, but not even that wounded me or humiliated me, because the memory of your suffering left no room for any other feelings. I rose slowly to my feet and made ready to challenge him, to soften his hardness and to throw down that wall by dint of weeping. But when my eyes met his I realized in a flash that the tone in which he had spoken of 'house-dogs' meant there were breaches in the wall. And it was your face, my daughter, that pushed me to climb in through one of them.

I gave the riposte to his argument: Did there have to be a before and after? Why couldn't children and dogs be looked after at the same time?[12] And while I was talking, I got the strange impression that you had begun to matter even more to him than you could to me, and that a flood of compassion was going out from him to you, sweeping away every dam, every obstacle, every defence in its path. I'll never be able to explain to you what it was about him that encouraged me to speak to him as an equal, or the strange power that emanated from him and made me feel the freedom of not being tied to any racial or religious hierarchy, any rules of cleanliness or legality. It was as if the two of us were already sitting round the table we were talking about, with bread being shared out among children and house-dogs and all the dividing lines between us going up in smoke, like the start of something absolutely new.

'Go, go home,' he said to me, as though I should hurry back to embrace you, 'For your saying that, the demon has left your daughter.'

I ran back home and found you lying on your bed with the peaceful expression of someone who is resting after having won a battle. And so I began calling you Eunice, so that your name might always remind us of the victory that, between us, we had won."'[3]

That was what my mother told me, and I am sure that no one, however hard he tries, can rebuild the barriers which Jesus himself knocked down that day.'

When I stopped talking there was a heavy silence, which only Mark dared to break: 'Brothers, listening to Eunice put me in mind of the words Paul wrote to the Galatians: "In Christ Jesus you are all children of God through faith . . . There is no longer Jew or Greek, there is no longer slave or free, there is no longer male and female; for all of you are one in Christ Jesus."'[14]

I never saw him again, but I later learned that he had put the episode he had heard from my lips into his Gospel. I was glad to see that it preceded by Jesus' discussion with the Pharisees about what can and cannot make people unclean[15] and that he repeated the term 'unclean spirit' for the demon. Because I thought with a certain malice about what that did for all the famous prescriptions of Leviticus and the storm that the sentence 'Thus he declared all foods clean' was going to raise among the Judaizers.

I also like the way he began his account by saying that Jesus *anastás*, 'rose up' – the same term he used to speak of the resurrection,[16] as though he were saying that the prejudices of separateness or superiority were another tomb that could not hold Jesus.

I was glad he made my mother say 'Lord', which we *Christians* (that lovely name that was first used in the community in Antioch)[17] use to address Jesus. And when I later had the whole Gospel in my hands, I saw that only she and Bartimaeus, the blind man who became a follower, call Jesus that.

But what really touched me was that he kept the words with which Jesus placed the power to save me in her – 'for saying that'. I have often asked myself what it was that he found in what she said, and why that became a highroad along which his healing power could travel. And from what I have since heard and learned about him, I believe that what amazed him was to find in a foreign woman such a deep affinity with his own passion for welcoming and including, for making the table shared with people on the margins one of the chief signs of his kingdom.

She challenged him to cross the one frontier he still had to cross and called him from the other side, where we still lived like a herd of sheep lost in the fog. And he must have heard in her voice an echo of his Father's voice and decided to cross.

That is why we can now sit at his table and nobody can deprive us of this place that is now open to all.[18] I was one of the first to be invited, and now I carry within me that same passion I inherited from my mother and learned from Jesus: to go on widening the space at that table until there is room for all those whose access is still barred to sit at it.

That's what I want to dedicate my life to, word of Eunice.

With the grace of him who won the victory for us over the powers of exclusion and death. *Chaire.*

Translated by Paul Burns

Notes

1. In this 'meditation' on the Syrophoenician woman I will use a hermeneutic of creative imagination, re-creating the narrative thread and re-reading the account in Mark from the viewpoint of its feminine protagonists. 'This type of hermeneutic seeks to articulate alternative interpretations, approaching the biblical text with the aid of historical imagination, narrative amplifications and artistic re-creations' (E. Schüssler Fiorenza, *But She Said. Feminist Practices of Biblical Interpretation,* New York 1976).

2. Ezek. 27.4.

3. Isa. 23.8.

4. Deut. 7.1–2.

5. Acts 11.19.

6. It is still significant for the history of the church that it was the groups most 'faithful to tradition' that ended outside the ecclesial communion, dispersed into sectarian tendencies – Ebionites, Encratites, etc.

7. Acts 11.1–4.

8. Isa. 23.16

9. Acts 10.23–8.

10. Mark uses the expression *pneuma akatharton*, 'unclean spirit', and this Greek adjective is what the Septuagint uses to translate the Hebrew *niddah*, 'impurity', meaning anything outside the sphere of the divine.

11. Cf V. Taylor, *The Gospel according to St Mark,* London 1952 *ad loc.* Rabbinic documentation in Billerbeck, I, 722–6.

12. Cf M. Navarro, 'La mujer y los límites', in *Misión Abierta* 8, 1992, 42.

13. 'During a heated debate between Jews and the academy of Jabneh, the Lord intervened in support of Rabbi Eliezer's position. But Rabbi Jehoshua protested, saying; "The Torah is not in heaven but here below!" And the majority voted against the opinion that had come down from heaven. Later Rabbi Nathan asked the prophet Elijah: "How did the Lord react to seeing that Rabbi Jehoshua took away, so to speak, his right to have the say?" Elijah answered: "The Lord smiled and said *Nitzkouni banai*, my sons have got the better of me"' (E. Wiesel, *Célébration prophétique*, Paris 1998, 186).

14. Gal. 3.26–28.

15. Mark 7.1–23.

16. Mark 8.31; 9.9; 10.31; 10.14 (but not in 7.1–39 in the standard English translations - *Trans.*).

17. Acts 11.26.

18. 'When Paul argued in favour of the meal in common with Christians of pagan origin he was making God's universal salvific will clear: God, in effect, wants to celebrate a banquet with everyone (Isa. 25.6; Luke 14.21). The church of the future needs to make this will even clearer if it is not to betray its Lord. Instructed by the letter to the Galatians, it is legitimate to state that the essence of Christianity is *synesthiein*, eating together' (F. Mussner, *Der Galaterbrief*, Freiburg 1974, 423).

The Church and the Crossing of Frontiers

Vimal Tirimanna

By her essential missionary nature, the church is called to cross frontiers, to proclaim the good news to all nations. In the process, this frontier crossing, from the point of view of the church, is always an entering into non-Christian 'territory'. In history, the opposite is also true: due to various historical factors, non-Christians, too, have crossed the frontiers and entered into church 'territory'. In all such frontier crossings, the common phenomenon has been the encounter of Christians and non-Christians (whether they were Muslims, Jews, Hindus, Buddhists or any of the other so-called 'pagans'). The consequences of such encounters, from the point of view of the church, have been both positive and negative. In a short, limited article of this nature, one cannot expect to deal with all the encounters of Christians and non-Christians in history, or with all the positive and negative consequences which ensued from them. One can only highlight a few, selected important encounters which have produced lasting positive or negative impacts. Accordingly, I shall divide this article into two main parts: I. The commission 'to go out'; II. A few important frontier crossings in the history of the church.

I. The commission 'to go out'

One of the main themes repeated throughout the Gospel of John is that Jesus is *sent* by God the Father, and that Jesus, in his turn, is *sending* his disciples to the world (cf. John 17.18). The climax of this Johannine sending is when the risen Christ breathes his Spirit on his disciples and *sends* them out (John 20.21). All the Synoptics have this commission 'to go out', but it is typically highlighted at the end of Matthew. 'All

authority in heaven and earth has been given to me. Go therefore and
make disciples of all nations, baptizing them in the name of the Father,
and of the Son and of the Holy Spirit, teaching them to observe all that I
commanded you; and lo, I am with you always, even to the end of time'
(Matt. 28.18–20). It is difficult to think of any other scripture passage
which has more influenced millions of Christians to be missionary, to go
out, to cross the frontiers in order to preach the good news about Jesus
Christ to the non-Christians or the so-called 'pagans', 'heathen' or
'infidels'. For them, it was simply the commission of the Lord himself to
cross the frontiers.

Basically, the above gospel passages together with the other relevant
New Testament writings not only stressed the importance of sharing the
Christ experience with those who have not yet heard it, but also
underlined that salvation was possible only through the one mediator,
Jesus the Christ. Thus Peter, filled with the Holy Spirit, tells the elders
and rulers of Jerusalem: 'There is salvation in no one else, for there is no
other name under heaven given among men by which we must be saved'
(Acts 4.12.) In his letter to Timothy, Paul says that God desires all men
and women to be saved and that this saving takes place only through
Christ Jesus, the mediator between God and man (I Tim. 2.4,5). In other
words, the desire to preach the good news and the need to save the
'infidels' from eternal damnation prompted many zealous men and
women to be *sent out*, 'to go out', to cross the frontiers. It should be
clear that this sense of being *sent out* is an essential element of the
church's very existence.

That the very essence of the church's mission is to go out and preach is
manifested in most of the church's magisterial documents. For example,
in 1919 Pope Benedict XV in his encyclical *Maximum Illud* gives a brief
history of the church's mission to the non-Christians from apostolic
times and calls it the noblest task of the church. He talks about the state
of the number of heathens or the infidels, who are still sitting in the
shadow of death. The Pope exhorts Christians in their missionary zeal to
forget about their own countries and to go out and evangelize, for they
are not enrolled citizens of any worldly state, but they need to get
enrolled in the heavenly state.

The traditional basic missionary thrust was upheld by the Second
Vatican Council, especially in the document *Ad Gentes* (1965) and by all
the subsequent magisterial documents on the mission of the church, such
as *Evangelii Nuntiandi* (1975) of Paul VI and *Redemptoris Missio* (1990)
of John Paul II. The commission 'to go out' and proclaim the good news
was stressed by all of them. However, as we shall notice in the following

section, the term 'frontier crossing' that was implied by these post-conciliar magisterial teachings took on an essentially different connotation.

II. A few important frontier crossings in the history of the church

1. The apostolic era

How the early church led by the apostles set about frontier crossing to announce the good news is clearly seen in the Acts of the Apostles. Briefly stated, it is full of missionary journeys, and in almost all these journeys, it is the Holy Spirit who prompts people to 'go out' (Acts 13.1–6; 19.21, etc.). Thus, we read of the Holy Spirit guiding the apostles to cross the frontier between the Jews and the Gentiles, as in the case of Philip in Acts 8 and Peter in Acts 10. The same Spirit guides them from place to place, forbidding them to preach in Asia or enter Bithynia, but giving them clear instructions to cross over to Europe (Acts 16.6–10). Of all those early apostolic missionary journeys, the journeys of Paul are second to none both in their vivid descriptions found in the New Testament and in their missionary zeal. Needless to say, these Pauline missionary journeys consisted of many frontier crossings. Some traditions hold that some apostles like Thomas went as far as India, crossing many frontiers.

In the process, the apostolic church not only fulfilled its mission of proclaiming the good news, but she also encountered the non-Jewish cultures and religions in Asia Minor, Northern Africa and Europe, which were predominantly Hellenistic or Roman. These encounters both enriched the church and at times corrupted her message. For example, the church was able to use some of the Greek concepts to express her message better, and at times, her message got contaminated by certain prevailing movements like Gnosticism. In the last analysis, however, the church's entrance into Europe marked a major turning point in history:

> When Paul, in obedience to the warning of a dream, set sail from Troy in AD 49 and came to Philippi in Macedonia he did more to change the course of history than the great battle that had decided the fate of the Roman Empire on the same spot nearly a century earlier, for he brought to Europe the seed of new life which was ultimately destined to create a new world.[1]

Thus it is important to note that during the very lifetime of the apostles themselves, the church was involved in frontier crossings in the process of her mission, which at times enabled her to enhance her message. However, at times such encounters also stunted, if not contaminated, the original vigour of the message.

2. The era of the great European missionaries

As the successors of the apostolic church, in obedience to the commission 'to go out and preach the good news', continued to cross frontiers, they encountered various nations, cultures, belief systems, etc. This is especially apparent in the writings of the Fathers of the church. It is important to note here that most of the Fathers themselves were 'pagan' converts to Christianity, which implies that when entering the church, they brought with them some of their non-Christian beliefs, philosophies and ways of life. A case in point is St Augustine (354–430) and his Manichean tendencies, which were manifested in his theology, especially his theology of sexuality and marriage. Similarly, some other Fathers were trying to use some of the philosophies with which they were familiar: this is how Platonic and Stoic philosophies, for example, crossed the frontiers into the church. Consequently, most of Christian thinking, especially Christian ethics, came to be conditioned by these 'pagan' philosophies. This was also the way in which some of the heresies entered the church. But, as the history of the church shows, it was precisely in confronting heresies that the doctrine of the church often developed. In this sense, such frontier crossings were beneficial to the church.

Although after their conversion some of the Fathers were accommodating and tolerant towards those who did not share the same Christian world-view, the majority of them clearly showed a sense of intolerance and even superiority. The absolute belief that Jesus Christ is the one and only saviour, and the divine mandate to proclaim this belief, seem to have prompted such negative attitudes towards those outside the church.

From the fifth century onwards, the great movements of the so-called 'barbarian tribes', who lived outside the Roman Empire, took place. They often crossed the frontiers of the church patronized by the imperial rulers since the time of Constantine in 313. In her turn, the church, too, ventured into the 'pagan' or 'barbarian' territories in the form of missionaries. Within the European continent, persons like Saints Patrick (385–461), Boniface (673–754), Cyril (died 869) and Methodius (died 885) were the leading missionaries who crossed into new non-Christian territories, to convert those who had not known Christ. It is important to note here that the first concern of most of these missionaries was to act primarily in the spirit of church unity and to derive their mission from that unity. This way, they felt that they were being 'sent by the Pope' to cross the frontiers. For example, after 719 Boniface acted as the ambassador of St Peter. In the process, such missionaries made sure that uniformity in church life, especially in doing what the church of Rome did, prevailed. Monastic life, especially that of St Benedict, helped the missionaries further not only in educating the newly converted tribes in the Christian way of life but also in ensuring that all of them acquired it in a uniform fashion. In short, these numerous types of encounters between the church and the 'barbarians' resulted in a new culture with the Latin Christian mark on it:

> Thus, there arose an autonomous Christian culture centring in the monasteries and permeating the Church and the life of the people by educational and religious influence. It was no longer a question of the conquering barbarians being affected by the religion and culture of the conquered, as with the Franks and Goths: it was a new creation produced by the grafting of the Latin Christian tradition on the native barbarian stock, so that it became internally assimilated by the new peoples.[2]

The triumph of Constantine and the subsequent Edict of Milan in 313 paved the way for another type of frontier crossing with regard to the church. Not only did Christianity gradually become the state religion, but the church also became the recipient of many civil privileges. In the process, civil authority crossed the frontiers of the church, and subsequently began to have many positive and negative effects on church life. Henceforth, church life would never be the same again, for church and state became closely interlinked. When a few centuries later the Empire began to disintegrate, fresh attempts were made to revive it, especially through the Carolingian renaissance. This renaissance, which was inaugurated by the emperor Charlemagne (768–814), gave further impetus to the missionaries to do 'as the Roman Church does it'. Charlemagne began the adoption of the liturgy of the city of Rome throughout the Empire and so indirectly and gradually throughout the entire Western Church. Some authors hold that the West as a unit with a common history began to exist only in the eighth century on the united basis of Roman liturgy, Roman canon law and Benedictine monasticism.[3]

3. The medieval era

During the high Middle Ages, there were two great events which saw important frontier crossings: 1. The emergence of Islam in the seventh century and its swift frontier crossing from Arabia to the Holy Land, and then across North Africa to the Iberian peninsula and the other European states surrounding the Mediterranean in 711; 2. The church's subsequent frontier crossing into Syria and the Latin Empire of Constantinople, from twelfth century onwards, in the form of Crusades. The phenomenon of Islam, which claimed to be God's definitive fulfilment of what God had wanted to communicate to 'the peoples of the book', namely, the Jews and Christians, posed a formidable challenge for the first time to the church's claim of absolute fulfilment of all God's promises in the person of Jesus Christ. Many contemporary theologians took up the challenge of this new religion, and as a result, Christian theology evolved further; the well known *Contra Gentiles* was Thomas Aquinas' response to this challenge, a few centuries later.

These Islamic invasions into the European Mediterranean basin and the Iberian peninsula, which later extended into the Pyrenees and southern France, also opened a new highway not only for various trade activities but also for cultural, philosophical and educational exchanges. Through the medieval schools of Salerno, Montpellier and Toledo, and the court of Palermo in Sicily, Greek and Arabic sciences and philosophies reached the Western world. It was precisely from these channels that the medieval culture of the thirteenth and fourteenth centuries derived its knowledge of Aristotle. The scholars of southern Italy and Spain translated into Latin the whole Aristotelian corpus in its Arabic form. The Aristotelian tradition was represented in its purest and most uncompromising form by the teaching of the Spanish Muslim Averroes, whose works were translated after 1217. During this period, there arose a great movement of co-operation, which took a cosmopolitan character: Jews, Arabs and Greeks co-operated with Spaniards, Italians and Englishmen, which implies a positive effect of frontier crossings.[4] It is also important to note here how much Aristotelian philosophy influenced medieval Christian theology, which went on to lay the basis for church life even to our day.

Within a few centuries of the Islamic invasion of Christian Europe, the church felt the need to regain her lost territories, especially in the Holy Land, and the means she employed to do this was to wage Crusades. Basically the Crusades were European military expeditions organized by the church for the liberation of the Holy Land and the defence of Christians living there. Such military activity against the invading Islamic forces came to be considered as works of piety after the ninth century. In fact, in 878, Pope John VIII promised absolution of their sins to troops who died while defending Christians against the Muslims who were then invading southern Italy. In 1063, Pope Alexander II granted the same favour to those Christians who died while fighting against the invading Muslims in Spain. With the declaring of the first

Crusade in 1095, the subsequent popes granted similar spiritual and temporal privileges to those Christian militants who took part in Crusades. Thus, in medieval Crusades, we notice a peculiar phenomenon which involved frontier crossings on the part of the church not to proclaim the good news as such (as it used to be in her previous frontier crossings), but to defend the Christian territories and the Christians who lived in them.

4. The colonial era

What we call 'the colonial era' began with *Inter cetera* of Pope Alexander VI in 1493, in which 'with the authority Almighty God has granted us' he entrusted the new world to the two kings of the Iberian peninsula and their successors 'for all time', so that they might 'subjugate the barbarian peoples and bring them to the faith'. It is interesting to note in the last phrase quoted above that the main purpose of the division of the new world between Spain and Portugal was to bring the 'barbarian peoples' in those lands 'to the faith'. To achieve this, the two Iberian powers were commissioned to cross the borders of the new world. This was the beginning of the European colonization of the rest of the world. Unfortunately, however, at least in the mind of those colonizers, the mission was not limited merely to converting 'barbarians' to the faith, but was coupled with other secular motives such as conquering nations for their own political and commercial gains. Thus, crossing frontiers to announce the good news during this era was closely associated with the colonial political powers, and this is precisely how the colonized peoples perceived their colonizers. The missionaries were hand in hand with the colonial political powers. It is no exaggeration to say that the colonial powers came with a sword in one hand and a Bible in the other:

> Whatever the intention of the messengers of the faith, missions looked like the other face of colonialism to the native peoples. Soldiers who conquered territory, merchants who exploited it, missionaries baptizing and founding schools – all came from the same country, had the same colour skin, spoke the same language and exchanged hospitality. No one could seriously doubt that they were all part and parcel of the same commodity.[5]

There is no doubt that it was mainly due to the tireless efforts of the European missionaries that the gospel message crossed the borders of many Asian, African and Latin American nations. Nor would one deny that those missionaries were men and women of their times, and often did the things they did in the missions with good, pure intentions. But on the other hand, most of them were trying to transplant European churches into their new local missionary contexts, often without any adaptation or contextualization. Consequently, the churches thus planted were 'alien' to the locals; to be precise, they were European in essence. The missionary attitude towards other great religions, especially in Asia, was also badly wanting. In a word, their entire missionary thrust was triumphalistic. However, there were a few enlightened missionaries who tried to enter the local contexts and thus adapt the gospel message to local attitudes and needs. Roberto di Nobili (1577–1656) in India, Joseph Vaz (1651–1711) and Giacome Gonzalvez (1705–1742) in Sri Lanka and Matteo Ricci (1552-1610) in China are a few such examples.[6] But most of these scattered efforts met with resistance and ended up with not much success. For our purposes, however, we need to notice that in the process, it was not the gospel of Jesus that crossed the frontiers of the new world during the period of colonization, but the gospel of Jesus clothed in European dress. According to Buhlmann, missionary activity and colonization have gone together almost throughout the history of the church's frontier crossings:

> For the Church's mission, it is a new experience to be facing the new nations. With a few exceptions, missionary activity has gone hand in hand with colonization for almost two millennia. No matter how we interpret the underlying relation between the two orders, it is self-evident that political expansion and the Church's expansion in the world have covered the same ground, geographically and chronologically. The cradle of Christianity was in Palestine, a Roman colony. In the first centuries the new religion spread along the roads of the Roman empire. Later, it spread throughout the colonial realms of Spain and Portugal.[7]

5. The era of inter-religious dialogue

The greatest ecclesial event in the twentieth century, the Second Vatican Council, while emphasizing the essential missionary thrust of the church to cross frontiers in proclaiming her message of good news, also gave clear guidelines for the ensuing encounters with different cultures, religions, philosophical systems, . . . etc. It clearly rejected the pre-Vatican-II missionary attitude of triumphalism and the resulting confrontations with everything non-Christian. Instead it encouraged dialogue.[8] The radical conciliar changes in the way the church understood such basic interrelated Christian concepts connected to her mission as salvation, the mediatorship of Christ, conversion, and true and false religion, also enhanced Christian efforts to engage in dialogue with the non-Christians. No longer does the church speak about 'the church and the world'; instead she now speaks about the 'church in the world', which itself implies a change of attitude. It is not a question of giving up her essential missionary mandate to proclaim the good news to all nations, but rather of engaging in dialogue with one another and sharing God with each other. In this conciliar missionary approach, the physical or geographical border crossing does not feature prominently; instead, relating to one another through mutual understanding and sharing God with each other becomes more important. Perhaps this may be regarded as a new way of frontier crossing by the church in proclaiming the good news.

This new missionary approach has been followed by almost all the post-Vatican-II magisterial documents. The documents of the Federation of Asian Bishops' Conferences (FABC), for example, continue to derive inspiration from these magisterial teachings and, consequently, to promote such dialogues, especially in the context of the great Asian religions.[9] Inter-religious dialogue is regarded by many Asian bishops as the appropriate way to proclaim the good news in Asia, as was clearly expressed by some of them at the recent Synod for Asia in Rome. In their response to the synodal preparatory document, the *lineamenta*, the bishops of Malaysia, Singapore and Brunei said: 'The Church can, like the Asian religions, learn to be more open, receptive, sensitive, tolerant, and forgiving in the midst of a plurality of religions.'[10]

III. Conclusion

From our brief and rather incomplete discussion above, it should be clear that the church by her very nature is missionary, is called to cross frontiers. From our selected historical outline, it should also be obvious that in such frontier crossings the church has often been interacting with other religions, cultures, philosophical systems, etc. In and through almost all such interactions, the church has been enriched in one way or the other, by the effects, both positive and negative, which ensued. The opposite is also true: the church has also been the cause of enrichment for others, outside her boundaries. However, due to her over-zealous missionary thrust, at times she has been very intolerant of all those who have refused to let her have her own way. The Second Vatican Council stressed the importance of checking such tendencies to be triumphalistic on the part of the church. Since then, the church's missionary endeavours would never be the same. For the church began to realize that she lived in a pluralistic society in which mutual harmony and co-existence are essential. It is in this sense that we are reminded of what the Jewish rabbi Abraham Heschel wrote:

> The religions of the world are no more self-sufficient, no more independent, no more isolated than individuals or nations. Energies, experiences and ideas that come to life outside the boundaries of a particular religion or all religions continue to challenge and to affect every religion.
>
> Horizons are wider, dangers are greater. *No religion is an island.* We are all involved with one another.[11]

In our contemporary world, we are all involved with one another. In this sense, our frontier-crossing can be a moment of grace when we encounter one another. Such encounters need to make us listen to one another, learn and unlearn from one another and even correct one another. For no one, not even a religion, is an independent, self-sufficient island. God uses each of us to speak to the other, especially in and through our frontier crossings and the ensuing encounters.

Notes

1. Christopher Dawson, *Religion and the Rise of Western Culture*, New York 1958, 27.

2. Ibid., 51f.

3. See, for example, Klaus Schatz, *Papal Primacy: From Its Origins to the Present*, Minnesota 1996, 68.

4. Cf. Dawson, *Religion* (n.1), 189–93.

5. Walbert Buhlmann, *The Coming of the Third Church,* Maryknoll 1982, 43.

6. For a concise but substantial discussion of this issue, cf. Hubert Jedin and John Dolan (eds.), *History of the Church: The Church in the Age of Absolutism and Enlightenment*, Vol. VI, London and New York 1981, 232–321.

7. Buhlmann, *Third Church* (n.5), 42.

8. Cf. *Nostra Aetate*, 2; *Ad Gentes*, 11; and *Gaudium et Spes* 92.

9. See, for example, the 'Final Declaration and Some Recommendations' of the First Plenary Assembly of the Federation of the Asian Bishops' Conferences (FABC) held in Taipei in 1974, Nos. 8–9, 13–17.

10. As cited in *The Tablet*, 2 May 1998, 571.

11. Abraham Joshua Heschel, 'No Religion is an Island', in *Christianity through Non-Christian Eyes,* ed. Paul J. Griffiths, Maryknoll 1990, 28, 29.

Mysticism as the Crossing of Ultimate Boundaries: A Theological Reflection

Wayne Teasdale

It is inevitably and invariably difficult to write about mystical experience and the whole inner process of contact with the Divine, or Ultimate Reality; it is completely surrounded by mystery. This difficulty is compounded when we try to speak about mysticism theologically. Most theological topics deal with issues that have been ostensibly settled by the church in councils, the magisterium, papal encyclicals, and sound theological studies. Naturally there is considerable difference of opinion among theologians, but a lot of agreement as well. When it comes to mysticism, however, it's not quite as easy. The reason is clear: the ineffability of mystical, contemplative or transcendental experience. Theologically, this quality of ineffability, of incomprehensibility or ungraspableness is a result of two related factors: the limitations of the human subject/knower and the experiential nature of mysticism as directly engaging the person within the depths of his/her subjectivity. The Divine Reality is infinite actuality and is eternal being, while the human person has an infinite potential, but only a finite experience. The ontological gap between the Divine and the human is unbridgeable from our side. Left to our own intellectual devices, we can never keep up with God, and we are always trying to catch up. Now when we add to this situation the experience of other traditions, things become very interesting; the potential for confusion is also very high. In what follows, I want to explore what I call *interspirituality* as a way of naming the phenomenon of crossing-over boundaries that mysticism makes possible and concrete. Substantial common ground exists among the various forms of spirituality scattered among the world's religions. The mystical and practical common ground will be identified, and then theological implications mentioned. We begin by considering the origin and nature of mysticism itself.

The origin and nature of mysticism

Every authentic religion derives from the primary spiritual realizations and experience of the founders. By authentic I mean arising out of the depths of our encounter with the Ultimate Mystery, the Divine Reality in its essential hiddenness, rather than merely invented by a disturbed individual. Hinduism, or the *Sanatana Dharma*, the Eternal Religion, as it is called, can be traced back to the *rishis*, the forest sages, or mystics of Indian antiquity. The Buddhist *Dharma* had its beginnings in the enlightenment event of Siddhartha Gautama, Sakyamuni, the Buddha, the Enlightened One. His life is paradigmatic of the inner spiritual process for every true Buddhist. Jainism arises out of the inner realizations of Mahavira and his twenty-three predecessors, and Mahavira himself was a contemporary of the Buddha, while Judaism was born out of a process of revelation from God to Abraham, Isaac, Jacob, Moses and the Prophets. Revelation is itself a mystical process with a corporate goal: to educate a people and then the whole of humankind in divine matters. In each of these instances, mysticism was the heart of their understanding. It is the same with Christianity and Islam. The Christian tradition rests on Jesus' inner awareness of his relationship with the Father, and Muhammad encountered Allah through the mediation of the Archangel Gabriel. All these religious traditions emerge out of mystical experience, and mystical experience means a direct knowledge of and relationship with the Divine, God, or boundless consciousness. One can almost say that the real *religion* of humankind isn't religion at all; rather, it is mystical spirituality, the bosom out of which the religions themselves have been born.

Mysticism is the awakening to and cultivation of transcendental consciousness. It is unitive awareness. All forms of mystical wisdom are unitive, that is, non-dual. They contribute to our deeper understanding of the mystery. This is a significant point of convergence among the religions themselves.[1] To say that mystical consciousness is unitive, non-dual, or integrative is simply to suggest that it points to an unusual state of awareness in which the person is united with God, Ultimate Reality; or, for the Buddhists, the person achieves absolute realization, an inner process of awakening to non-dual consciousness in which a changeless wisdom is activated.[2]

In mystical consciousness, the transcendent is touched, or is reached, and it touches, embraces us. Mystical consciousness means integration with it, and to know it directly with certainty, although it defies description. It can be experienced but not comprehended with any clarity, indeed not comprehended at all! We know, but we do not fully grasp, the Divine mystery. Encountering the transcendent reality confers on us a degree of knowledge, the knowledge that it *is*, that it *exists*, and a kind of wisdom that has a practical utility for our spiritual life. Mystical experience, however, is fleeting, though its fruits are lasting, often permanent. Some of the effects include: wisdom, deep peace or tranquillity, joy, compassion, patience, gentleness, selflessness and simplicity.

Interspirituality

Interspirituality[3] is a term to describe the breaking-down of the barriers that have separated the religions for millennia. It is also the crossing-over and the sharing in the spiritual, aesthetic, moral and psychological treasures that exist in the different traditions of spirituality living within the world religions. The deepest level of sharing is in and through one another's mystical wisdom, whether teachings, insights, methods of spiritual practice, and their fruits. The mystical life, in its maturity, is characteristically, naturally, even organically interspiritual because of the inner freedom and liberation the mystical journey ignites in the depths of the person. It frees us from the obstacles within us that would hold us back from that generosity and willingness to partake in the mystical springs of other traditions. To drink this precious nectar requires openness and a capacity to assimilate the depth experience of these venerable traditions. More and more it is becoming common for individuals to cross over the frontiers of their own faith into the land of another or others. So much is this the case that we can speak of this new millennial period as the Interspiritual Age. This development is momentous news for the human family, because up until this point humankind has been divided, segregated into spiritual ghettos. Out of this separation has come so much misunderstanding, and thousands of wars sparked by mutual suspicion, isolation, competition and hostility.

The Interspiritual Age promises to melt away the old barriers, and with them, the old antagonisms. This is one reason why it should be nurtured and encouraged. Interspirituality opens the way to friendship[4] among members of differing faiths. Friendship creates bonds of community[5] between and among the religions through their members, and community represents a shift from the old competitive, antagonistic model to a new opportunity, a new paradigm of relationship that seeks to meet on common ground. Community makes interspirituality possible, and the cross-over substantial. Transcendental experience awakens us to the possibility of radical spiritual change by allowing us to see beyond the boundaries that have kept us all separate from one another and isolated in our systems. The interspiritual development is a process of transcending boundaries, carrying us, and humanity also, to a new vision of life, one in which we live on the bridges that unite us, no longer in isolation. The bridge is our future, and that is an interspiritual vision. I believe it was the poet Kabir who likened life to a bridge, and admonished us not to build a house on it!

The common ground that interspirituality reveals is both in the reality of mystical experience itself and in the practical elements of the spiritual life in each tradition. In the mystical, transcendental sphere the basis of entering this realm of depth, height and breadth is consciousness itself. All traditions emphasize the deep interiority of the contemplative vision. This vision, or rather, direction, is a *sine qua non* for breakthroughs, discoveries, and real progress on our own journey. All mystical experience requires consciousness as a medium and as perceived reality of the Ultimate. The Divine modifies our consciousness so that we can be aware of it. Without consciousness there would be no mysticism.

On the mystical level there is an option between an intimate, personal, loving God, with whom we can enter into a profound relationship of love and knowledge in the embrace of divine union initiated by God, or the transpersonal, impersonal realization of the ultimate condition of mind, or consciousness of the Buddhist tradition. These two trajectories of mystical perception are available to us. Perhaps it is necessary for us to experience both of these ways, and that is what interspirituality challenges us to do. By so doing, we share in a much larger understanding of the Absolute, and have the opportunity to experience both the personal Divine and the transpersonal Source.

The practical dimension of interspirituality reveals to us the common ground among the traditions in those elements that are part of the mature expression of each tradition of spirituality in the lives of practitioners. If you take an example of an individual in each tradition of spirituality who has achieved a degree of genuine depth and transformation, the elements in each instance will be the same. These include an actualized capacity to live the moral life, a deep commitment to non-violence, a simplicity of life-style, a sense of one's interconnectedness with all living beings and the earth itself, a spiritual practice like prayer, meditation, contemplation, along with liturgy, self-knowledge in which we see ourselves as we are, compassionate service, and a commitment to justice, or prophetic witness and action. Even a cursory glance around the traditions will demonstrate the value of this observation.

Theological implications of mysticism

If the mystical experience of other traditions is genuine and if it is on the same level as Christian contemplation in its fullness in the transforming union, the spiritual marriage between God and the soul, then one implication is that Christianity does not have a monopoly on wisdom as it relates to the nature of the Divine. Christian theological formulations do not exhaust the infinite reality and subtlety of the Divine nature. This means that we can learn from the inner experience of other forms of spirituality. Christianity's understanding of God is not complete in this sense, nor is the experience and understanding of the other traditions complete without the Christian contribution. Buddhism, for example, needs the insight on the Divine, an insight won from thousands of years of mystical consciousness. Complementarity is thus the direction toward which the mystical leads us. In this way, humankind can cross the boundaries to reach the further shore of our eternal homeland.

Notes

1. Thomas Keating, an American Trappist who founded the Snowmass Conference, an interfaith group with fifteen members. Each member represents a world religion and is a spiritual teacher in it. Over the years, the Snowmass Conference has discovered points of agreement, and these they have formulated in a document called *Guidelines for Interreligious Understanding*; they relate primarily to the Ultimate Mystery. See *Speaking of Silence: Christians and Buddhists on the Contemplative Way*, ed. Susan Walker, New York 1987, 126-9.

2. The Tibetan tradition calls this *Dzogchen*, the perfected condition of the mind.

3. See my article, 'The Interspiritual Age: Practical Mysticism for the Third Millennium', *Journal of Ecumenical Studies* 34.1, Winter 1997.

4. The Dalai Lama has often remarked that inter-religious dialogue must be based on friendship between those who engage in this important work.

5. See *The Community of Religions: Voices and Images of the Parliament of the World's Religions*, ed. George Cairns and Wayne Teasdale, New York 1996.

From Exclusion to Embrace

Miroslav Volf

We live in a world of rampant exclusion. Sometimes we exclude by abandoning, sometimes by dominating, sometimes by assimilating; in extreme cases we exclude by eliminating. Often the practice of exclusion is justified by a rich language of exclusion and sustained by a range of negative emotional responses to others, from hatred to indifference. It seems that exclusionary practices, language and emotional responses come easy to us, way too easy. What is difficult is to walk the road of mutual embrace that will let others live in communion with us, indeed that will foster their flourishing. I want to explore what it takes to practice embrace in a world of exclusion. I will first explore two dominant metaphors for regulating social life and then suggest how the prevalent understanding of social covenant might be enriched so as to foster embrace.

Contract[1]

One powerful contemporary metaphor for social life is the metaphor of 'contract'. Political liberalism, which conceives life as essentially a business of individual self-interest, has promoted 'contract' as the master metaphor of social life. Plagued by fear of harm and driven by desire for comfort, individuals enter into 'contracts' which favour them with 'security and gain'.[2] Contracts let each achieve with the help of others what none could achieve alone. Civil society emerges as the offspring of such contractual interaction. Are the shoulders of 'contract' broad enough, however, to carry the social burden placed on it?

Consider the following three notable features of contracts. First, they are *performance-orientated*. Though conviviality may be a pleasant side-benefit, the point of a contract is to ensure that a task is accomplished, say, a commodity produced or a service rendered. The task done, the relationship dissolves – in so far as it was regulated by contract. Second, contracts are marked by *limited commitment*. In the words of Philip Selznick,

> terms and conditions are specified closely, and the cost of non-performance is calculable. Furthermore, with some exceptions, the moral or legal obligation is not necessarily *to fulfil* the agreement, but only to make good losses that may be incurred in case of an unjustified breach.[3]

The contract obliges only to what it explicitly or implicitly states, no less and certainly no more. Third, contract is strictly *reciprocal*. The consent of both parties is needed to oblige both; obversely, the transgression of the one dis-obliges the other. In an important sense, the contract is designed to make the parties mirror each other's behaviour. As Bauman puts it, 'the "duty to fulfil the duty" is for each side dependent on the other side's record. I am obliged to abide by the contract only as long, and in as far, as the partner does the same.'[4]

Given the contract's strict reciprocity, limited commitment and performance-orientation it is easy to see why it would emerge as the master metaphor for social relations in contemporary societies. In a typically modern way, our lives are organized around the roles we play, and we like to think that we are free to choose which roles to play and how long to play them. We offer services in exchange for services, but keep our opinions open for a better deal or a more desirable benefit. Contracts make relations binding but not inflexible; they commit without enslaving. Tailor-made for interaction between social actors who see themselves as separate units and whose most sacred good is freedom to decide what they want and how long they want it, contracts both stabilize commitments and keep them fluid. They seem the perfect structuring principle of an order typical of contemporary societies, always 'local, emergent and transitory'.[5]

The social utility of contracts is indisputable; without them life in detraditioned and differentiated societies would be nearly impossible. But will 'contract' do as the master metaphor for social life as a whole? Can it offer more than just a 'descriptive code' for what we do in one important segment of our lives? Does it suggest a vision of how we should live, a vision of the good life? Hardly. In a contractual model of society, the three salient features of contracts are three important ways of misconstruing human life. First, human beings are not 'autonomous individuals' who associate only to perform tasks that advance their self-interests; relations to other people penetrate below the surface of the self.

To give but one example, even with a contract in hand, a patient wants more from a doctor than competent technical performance; functional relations between them feed on 'irrational' and non-specific emotional bonds. Second, at many levels mutual commitments cannot be limited by terms and conditions clearly specified in advance. Often human beings are bound by something like a common 'destiny', not just by mutual utility. As the example of divorce shows (even a 'successful' one), it is impossible strictly speaking 'to make good losses' incurred by a breach of such intimate fellowship. Finally, we have obligations to our neighbours that are not invalidated by our neighbour's failure to fulfil corresponding obligations to us; our relationships are not strictly reciprocal. If my neighbour breaks trust, I am not entitled to do the same, as I would be entitled not to pay her for a service she did not render. As the master metaphor for social relations, 'contract' is deeply flawed because human beings are socially situated, their lives intertwined, and their interchange morally 'encumbered'.

Covenant

Troubled by the dominance of contractual relations in contemporary societies 'which leave every commitment unstable'[6] and undermine community, some social philosophers have advocated retrieval of 'covenant' as the alternative master metaphor of social life. With its original home in the world of religious commitments rather than business transactions, 'covenant' promises better to express the communal and moral dimensions of human life. In contrast to 'contract', Selznick argues in *Moral Commonwealth*, 'covenant'

> suggests an indefeasible commitment and a continuing relationship. The bond is relatively unconditional, relatively indissoluble . . . The bond contemplates open-ended and diffuse obligations, implicates the whole person or group, and creates a salient status.[7]

A 'communitarian liberal', Selznick refuses to give up either on the modern 'autonomous individual'[8] or on the 'relatively unconditional' bonds and 'moral ordering' of social life.[9] 'Covenant,' he claims, allows him to hold on to both. It speaks both of autonomy and belonging, of individual commitments and ongoing social situatedness: 'covenant' contains 'vital elements of voluntarism and consent' and creates obligations which 'derive from the nature and history of the relationship' and cannot be 'fully specified in advance'.[10] Unlike contract, which defines a limited and reciprocal commitment, covenant structures an open-ended and morally ordered relationship.

But what is 'the nature of the relationship' that the covenant structures? What kind of common history does it create? Why should this relationship not be exclusive, for instance, designed to promote the interests of a 'community of destiny' that is morally ordered in deeply immoral ways? Was not apartheid based on the covenant idea too? Covenant may morally structure communal life, but the decisive question is surely what will morally structure the covenant itself so as to make it a covenant of justice rather than oppression, of truth rather than deception, of peace rather than violence. Selznick makes the principle that 'all men are created equal' the chief 'covenantal premise'. But he arrives at the principle not through the idea of covenant, but through 'a leap of faith', 'a self-defining commitment', 'a venture in constitution-making'. In other words, the theory of covenant works as 'a theory of moral ordering' only because he adds to the formal structure of the covenant as a pattern of social relations the commitment to certain 'self-evident principles'.[11] 'Covenant' has no moral feet of its own, but must rest on substantive values that come from elsewhere. These substantive values do much more social work than the formal notion of the 'covenant'.

In today's political discourse the notion of covenant draws much of its potency from the fact that the United States of America was 'a nation formed by a covenant'.[12] 'A covenant' could form 'a nation', of course, only because the so-called Calvinist 'monarchomachians' first formed a covenantal idea of nation. For them, however, the covenant of human beings with one another was 'based on and preserved by God's covenant with them'.[13] The covenant's moral feet were supplied by the covenant-making God. The duties of human beings as God's covenant partners were expressed in the 'moral law', the Decalogue, that federal theologians considered universally binding. It mapped a moral order that extended as far as the rule of the one God reached: it encompassed the whole of human community. Covenant could become a useful political category because it was first a moral category, and it became moral category because it was at its core a theological category. All particular human covenants, from family and neighbourhood to state, must be subordinate to the inclusive covenant that encompasses the whole of humanity and is guided by substantive values – the universal 'holding on to each other' in solidarity. Without some such universal substantive values to form its premises, covenant may well serve as the bond of political community, but the political community will be no better than the values it espouses;

by itself, the covenant will certainly not provide an adequate standard by
which a political community can judge itself.

Beyond the stress on the universality of covenant and the substantive
values stemming from God's covenant with humanity, what can theology
bring to the reflection about covenant as the master metaphor for social
life? In his article 'Covenant or Leviathan', Jürgen Moltmann has
followed the early federalist 'political theologians' and underscored the
freedom that people united by a covenant under God acquire to resist
'the great Leviathan' – a tyrannical government.[14] He analysed the
vertical relation of the covenanting people to the state; his concern was
the nature of consent and the limits of political authority. I want to
supplement his analysis by looking at the horizontal relation between the
covenanting people themselves: my concern is the nature of commitments and the conditions for communal flourishing.

'By mutual covenants one with another,' says Thomas Hobbes in
Leviathan, people transfer 'authority' to the state and thus give birth to
'that great Leviathan (or rather, to speak more reverently . . . *mortal
god*), to which we owe under the *immortal God*, our peace and defence'.[15]
The transfer of power in the moment of the unanimity of 'every man with
every man' is necessary to end the persisting war of 'everyone against
everyone'. Incapable of forming and keeping covenants between themselves, people need Leviathan so that by the 'terror' of his power and
strength he may 'form the wills of them all' and thereby ensure 'peace at
home and mutual aid against their enemies abroad'. Leviathan emerges
out of the murky and chaotic waters of negative anthropology. In
contrast, covenant presupposes a more positive anthropology. As
Moltmann has argued, trust in the God who enters into covenant with
human beings grounds the trust in their ability to form covenants.[16]

Yet the indisputable human capacity to make covenants is matched by
their incontestable capacity to break them. The cumulative message of
the biblical covenantal traditions is that both 'capacities' are in fact the
two intertwined ways of communal living: human beings continually
make and break covenants. And behind the tumult of 'making' and
'breaking' lies an anthropological constant: human beings are always
already in the covenant as those who have always already broken the
covenant. Reflection on the intricate dynamics of making and breaking
covenants should therefore supplement (not substitute!) the interest in
the alternative between negative and positive anthropology.

New covenant

For public theology, much more significant than the 'original covenant' on which the federalist tradition builds is the 'new covenant', which remains almost completely neglected as a resource for political thought. The new covenant, too, presupposes the capacity of humans to form covenants. Yet it situates this capacity in the midst of a history of conflict not simply between the people and the state, but among the covenanting people themselves. First, the new covenant is a response to a persistent pattern of breaking of the covenant. In social terms, it emerges against the backdrop of enmity, understood not as some fictive 'state of nature', to be rectified by an equally fictive 'covenant', but as a pervasive social dynamic between the people who already belong to the covenant but fail to keep it. Second, the new covenant raises the fundamental issue of how to transcribe the covenantal promises written on the 'tablets of stone' on to 'hearts of flesh' (Jer. 31.31ff.). Above and beyond persuading people to resist tyrants by entering and keeping covenants, a key political task must be to nurture people whose very identity should be shaped by the covenants they have formed so that they do not betray and tyrannize one another.

To place the new covenant at the centre of a public theology means for a Christian theologian to inquire about the relation between the cross and the covenant. On the cross we see what God has done to renew the covenant that humanity has broken. What can we learn from the cross about how to renew the covenant – renew in the triple sense of strengthening the covenants that are fragile, repairing the covenants that are broken, and keeping the covenants from being completely undone?

First, on the cross God renews the covenant by making space for humanity in God's self. The open arms of Christ on the cross are a sign that God does not want to be a God without the other – humanity – and suffers humanity's violence in order to embrace it. What could this divine 'making-space-in-oneself' imply for social covenants?

I argued earlier, agreeing with the critics of the contractual model of society, that unlike contract, covenant is not simply a relationship of mutual utility, but of moral commitment. But we have to go a step further. For the covenant partners are not simply moral agents who have certain duties to one another within the framework of a long-standing relationship. Precisely because covenant is lasting, the parties themselves cannot be conceived as individuals whose identities are external to one another and who are related to one another only by virtue of their moral will and moral practice. Rather, the very identity of each is formed through relation to others; the alterity of the other enters into the very identity of each.

Under these conditions, to renew the covenant means to 'transcend the perspective of the one side and take into account the complementary dispositions of the other side';[17] even more, to renew the covenant means to attend to the shifts in the identity of the other, to make space for the changing other in ourselves, and to be willing to re-negotiate our own identity in interaction with the fluid identity of the other. Each party in the covenant must understand its own behaviour and identity as complementary to the behaviour and identity of other parties. Without such complementarity and continual readjustments of dynamic identities, moral bonds will not suffice as protection against the pressure on the covenant, and the door will open for Leviathan's return.

Second, renewing the covenant entails self-giving. On the cross the new covenant was made 'in blood' (Luke 23.20). Notice that the blood of the new covenant was not the blood of a third party (an animal), shed to establish a fictive blood relation between the parties of the covenant and dramatize the consequences of breaking it. In this respect the new covenant is profoundly different from the first covenant God made with Abraham (Genesis 15). Abraham cut the sacrificial animals in two and 'a smoking fire pot and a flaming torch' – both symbols of theophany – passed between the halves (15.17). The unique ritual act performed by God was a pledge that God would rather 'die' than break the covenant, much as the animals through which God passed died. The thought of a living God dying is difficult enough – as difficult as the thought of a faithful God breaking the covenant. At the foot of the cross, however, a veritable abyss opens up for the thought. For the narrative of the cross is not a 'self-contradictory' story of a God who 'died' because God broke the covenant, but a truly incredible story of God doing what God should neither have been able nor willing to do – a story of God who 'died' because God's all too human covenant partner broke the covenant.

The 'blood' in which the new covenant was made is not simply the blood that holds up the threat of breaking the covenant or that portrays common belonging: it is the blood, but of self-giving, even self-sacrifice. The one party has broken the covenant and the other suffers the breach because it will not let the covenant be undone. If such suffering of the innocent party strikes us as unjust, in an important sense it *is* unjust. Yet the 'injustice' is precisely what it takes to renew the covenant. One of the biggest obstacles to repairing broken covenants is that broken covenants invariably entail deep disagreements over what constitutes a breach and who is responsible for it. Partly because of the desire to shirk the responsibilities that acceptance of guilt involves, those who break the covenant do not (or will not) recognize that they have broken it. In a world of clashing perspectives and strenuous self-justifications, of crumbly commitments and strong animosities, covenants are kept and renewed because those who, from their perspective, have not broken the covenant are willing to do the hard work of repairing it. Such work is self-sacrificial: something of the individual or communal self dies performing it. Yet the self by no means perishes, but is renewed as the truly communal self, fashioned in the image of the Triune God who will not be without the other.

Third, the new covenant is eternal. God's self-giving on the cross is a consequence of the 'eternality' of the covenant, which in turn rests on God's 'inability' to give up the covenant partner who has broken the covenant. 'How can I hand you over, O Israel?' asks rhetorically Hosea's God, whose 'compassion grows warm and tender' (11.8), because God is bound to Israel with 'bonds of love'. God's commitment is irrevocable and God's covenant indestructible. Analogously, though any given political covenant may be dissolved, being 'relatively unconditional',[18] the broader social covenant is strictly unconditional and therefore 'eternal'. It can be broken, but it cannot be undone. Every breach of the covenant still takes place within the covenant; and all the struggle for justice and truth on behalf of the victims of the broken covenant takes place within the covenant. Nobody is outside the social covenant; and no deed is imaginable which would put a person outside it.

Readjustment of complementary identities, repairing of the covenant by those who have not broken it, and refusal to let the covenant ever be undone – these are the key features of a social covenant conceived in analogy to a Christian theology of the new covenant. The three features correspond closely with what in my book *Exclusion and Embrace* I have called 'embrace' – a metaphor which seeks to combine the thought of reconciliation with the thought of dynamic and mutually conditioning identities. The new covenant is God's embrace of the humanity that keeps breaking the covenant; the social side of that new covenant is our way of embracing one another under the conditions of enmity. I said earlier that reflection on social relations from the perspective of the new covenant ('embrace') is not meant to replace but to supplement reflection from the perspective of the 'old covenant' (covenant). What is the relation between the two? Embrace is the inner side of the covenant, and covenant is the outer side of the embrace.

Notes

1. The following text is adapted from my book *Exclusion and Embrace: A Theological Exploration of Identity, Otherness and Reconciliation*, Nashville 1996, 147–56.

2. W. M. Sullivan, *Reconstructing Public Philosophy*, 1982, 13.

3. P. Selznick, *The Moral Commonwealth: Social Theory and the Promise of Community*, Berkeley 1992, 379.

4. Z. Bauman, *Postmodern Ethics*, Oxford 1993, 59.

5. Z. Bauman, *Intimations of Postmodernity*, London 1992, 189.

6. R. Bellah, R. Madsen, W. M. Sullivan, A. Swidler and S. M. Tipton, *Habits of the Heart: Individualism and Commitment in American Life*, New York 1985, 130.

7. Selznick, *Moral Commonwealth* (n.3).

8. Ibid., 482ff.

9. Ibid., 477.

10. Ibid., 480.

11. Ibid., 482f.

12. J. Schaar, *Legitimacy and the Modern State*, New Brunswick 1981, 291.

13. J. Moltmann, 'Covenant or Leviathan? Political Theology for Modern Times', *Scottish Journal of Theology* 47.1, 1994, 25.

14. Ibid., 19–40.

15. T. Hobbes, *Leviathan*, reissued Indianapolis 1967, Part 2, Ch. 17.

16. Moltmann, 'Covenant or Leviathan?' (n.13), 25.

17. A. and J. H. Assmann, 'Aspekte einer Theorie des unkommunikativen Handelns', in H. A. and D. Harth (eds), *Kultur und Konflikt*, Frankfurt am Main 1990, 36.

18. Selznick, *Moral Commonwealth* (n.3), 479.

III · Testimonies

Francis of Assisi. A Bridge to Islam

Anton Rotzetter

For various reasons, Francis of Assisi can be understood as a bridge between Christianity and Islam.

I. The historical encounter with Sultan Malik-al-Kamil

In 1212 Francis wanted to travel to Syria and in 1213 to Morocco. The first time stormy winds drove him to Dalmatia, according to tradition to Dubrovnik, and the second time he reached Santiago di Compostela on foot, but then had to return because of sickness. His motive was to proclaim the good news of Jesus to the Saracens,[1] as the Muslims or adherents of Islam were called in the Middle Ages, and if possible to give proof of it or suffer martyrdom.

A third journey was successful: on 29 August 1219 Francis witnessed the defeat of the Crusader army at Damietta in Egypt, which he foresaw and wanted to prevent. Following it, with his Franciscan brother Illuminatus he managed to make his way to Sultan Malik-al-Kamil (1218-1228), with whom he had a memorable encounter, a number of conversations which lasted several days. Jacques de Vitry,[2] Thomas of Celano[3] and other witnesses report that the Sultan was fascinated and impressed with Francis and afterwards had him escorted back to the Christian camp with full honour. According to other witnesses the Sultan even allowed him to visit the holy places and gave him an escort to do so. Moreover, Francis and his brothers were given a pass so that they could travel in Muslim areas. In Assisi, a horn given to Francis by the Sultan as a personal present is still on display. Francis used it whenever he wanted to send brothers out to preach the gospel.[4] Some writers think that this encounter was a missionary success. It was certainly that if measured by the motivations of the saint: Francis did not convert the Sultan and his followers, nor did he suffer martyrdom. But the encounter took place

within a framework which was already extraordinary given the circumstances at that time. So we can say that the encounter was successful in its
historical significance and symbolic content.

II. The new spirit of encounter

Granted, the twelfth century had already produced very impressive
evidence of cultural bridge-building. Thus for example Petrus Venerabilis (died 1156) formulated a programme[5] of non-violent, loving and
inviting encounter with the Saracens. His protégé Peter Abelard (died
1142) went much further with his fascinating vision of a 'Conversation
between a Philosopher, a Jew and a Christian',[6] even if he did not
expressly include Islam in his programme of dialogue. But this amazing
liberal spirit was then largely displaced by a series of Crusades,[7] and by
an aggressive spirit ready for violence. Thus for Francis's contemporaries
the Saracens were 'beasts', 'wolves', wild beasts who had to be met with
violence. Here opportunities for encounter and indeed for peace were
certainly missed. They were certainly there, as Sultan Malik-al-Kamil
shows. Domestic political rivalries and revolts, and also spiritual motives,
made him a man who met Christians with offers of a truce and peace, and
Francis with generosity.

The quite different framework in which the encounter between
Francis and the Sultan took place is evident in the 'mission statute'
which is incorporated in the *Regula non Bullata*[8] as its sixteenth chapter.
It is significant quite simply because for the first time in history the
notion of mission emerges in the rule of an order. The content[9] is quite
revolutionary:

1. The encounter with the Saracens is primarily to be one of pure
presence: serving, peaceful, non-violent, indeed obedient and subservi-
ent presence, which attests and confesses the Christian faith simply as
solidarity lived out between brothers and sisters.

2. However, the explicit preaching of the gospel is secondary. It may
take place only if an additional inner impulse, the recognized will of God,
is behind it.

3. This preaching is not limited to clerical and hierarchical actions.
Rather, it grows directly out of Christian existence itself and therefore
has primarily a lay character. For the statements with which Francis
describes explicit preaching in the statute on mission are structurally[10]
related to chapter 21[11] of the same rule. In it he speaks of the exhortation
and praise with which 'whenever they see fit, my friars may exhort the
people to praise God'.

4. The encounter with the Saracens is to be marked by total surrender. After describing the criteria for Franciscan encounter mentioned above, soberly and prosaically, Francis intensifies them in an ecstatic and mystical way. Here he refers to God's total surrender in Jesus Christ and to the response that he and his brothers are to make to it. They had already given themselves totally to God even before they went to the Saracens. So in the end they have nothing to fear. The Saracens can take nothing that they have not previously given. Thus the early Christian readiness for martyrdom is bound up with a motto of early Franciscan lifestyle: *contemplando se aliis tradere*, giving oneself into the hands of others in contemplation of God's total surrender of himself. That leads to courage, lack of fear, selflessness and forgetfulness of self in the encounter with the Saracens. In other words, for Francis a readiness for martyrdom is an essential part of the statute on mission. But that does not mean that one should provoke a martyr death. That would be in opposition to the first point above.

Because the statute on mission is so important for the encounter with other cultures, I shall quote it in full here (omitting only a few scriptural quotations which are more cosmetic):

Our Lord told his apostles: 'Behold, I am sending you forth like sheep in the midst of wolves. Be therefore wise as serpents, and guileless as doves' (Matt. 10.16). And so the friars who are inspired by God to work as missionaries among the Saracens and other unbelievers must get permission to go from their minister, who is their servant. The minister, for his part, should give them permission and raise no objection, if he sees that they are suitable; he will be held to account for it before God, if he is guilty of imprudence in this or any other matter.

The brothers who go can conduct themselves among them spiritually in two ways.

One way is to avoid quarrels or disputes and 'be subject to every human creature for God's sake' (I Peter 2.13), so bearing witness to the fact that they are Christians.

Another way is to proclaim the word of God openly, when they see that is God's will, calling on their hearers to believe in God almighty, Father, Son, and Holy Spirit, the Creator of all, and in the Son, the Redeemer and Saviour, that they may be baptized and become Christians, because 'unless a man be born again of water, and the Spirit, he cannot enter into the kingdom of God' (John 3.5).

They may tell them all that and more, as God inspires them, because our Lord says in the Gospel: 'Everyone who acknowledges me before men, I also will acknowledge him before my Father in heaven' (Matt. 10.32); and: 'Whoever is ashamed of me and my words, of him will the Son of Man be ashamed when he comes in his glory and that of the Father and of the holy angels' (Luke 9.26).

No matter where they are, the friars must always remember that they have given themselves up completely and handed over their whole selves to our Lord Jesus Christ, and so they should be prepared to expose themselves to every enemy, visible or invisible, for love of him. He himself tells us, 'He who loses his life for my sake will save it' (Mark 9. 35), for eternal life. 'Blessed are they who suffer persecution for justice' sake, for theirs is the kingdom of heaven' (Matt. 5.10).

III. The effects of the encounter on Francis and his brothers

Francis's encounter with the Saracens found great resonance in the Franciscan literature. We can only guess at the effects it had on Francis himself. But we can note:

1. Francis must have been very moved by the reverence with which Muslims worship Allah. In his letter to the order there are passages which recall the practice of prayer in Islam. 'At the sound of his name you should *fall to the ground* and adore him with fear and reverence . . . Incline the ear of your heart and obey the voice of the Son of God . . . This is the very reason he has sent you all over the world, so that by word and deed you might bear witness to his message and convince everyone *that there is no other almighty God beside him.*'[12] Here an understanding of God and a corresponding form of behaviour is evident, which cannot conclusively be attributed to experiences with Islam, but which perhaps can be explained specifically from that. Thus the so-called Thana, the song of praise which begins the worship of God, offered five times a day, runs: 'O God, to Thee be praise and glory; blessed is Thy Name and there is no God but Thee.'

It is particularly striking how Francis stands out by virtue of an unusual reverence for the name and the word Jesus. He even goes so far – in contrast, say, to papal statements in this connection, which will be mentioned shortly – as to accord the word pre-eminence over the sacrament: it is the word which makes the sacrament the sacrament; without the word the signs have no content and meaning.[13] 'The greatness of our creator and of our subjection to him'[14] is the abiding tenor of the letters which he wrote following the papal Brief *Sane cum olim* (1219) on his return from the East. Even if there should be no causal connection between this understanding of God and Islam, here we have in fact material for building a bridge between Christianity and Islam.

2. The Thana just mentioned is the beginning of the so-called Salat, the ritual prayer said five times a day which is called down from the minarets by the muezzin (in the morning, at noon, in the afternoon, at sunset and before going to sleep). Evidently Francis was so impressed by this that he also wanted to introduce something similar in Western society. He sees the great danger of faith withdrawing into the private sphere so that the public sphere can 'forget God . . . because of the cares and anxieties of this world'. Therefore he proposes to the 'rulers of the peoples' that they should enact appropriate legislation for the praise of God: 'See to it that God is held in great reverence among your subjects; every evening, at a signal given by a herald or in some other way, praise and thanks should be given to the Lord God almighty by all the people.'[15] Possibly Francis even assigns the function of the muezzin to his own brothers: 'When you are preaching, too, tell the people about the glory that is due to him, so that at every hour and when the bells are rung, praise and thanks may be offered to almighty God by everyone all over the world.'[16] 'Of the other letters that I send you to give to burgomasters, consuls and governors, in which it is said that the praise of God shall be proclaimed publicly among the people and in the squares, immediately make many copies and deliver them with great care to those to whom they are to be given.'[17] Here too what was said in connection with 1. above applies. There is no conclusive proof that Francis's ordinance is to be derived from the Islamic Salat, but a direct connection here is very probable. At all events, here too we can find a level of argument for a dialogue which goes beyond a particular religion.

3. The possible reference of the famous legend of the 'Wolf of Gubbio'[18] to the Saracens is also interesting. The place with which the legend is associated recalls a victory of the town of Gubbio over the Saracens,[19] and the statute on mission begins with the biblical quotation 'Behold, I am sending you forth like sheep in the midst of wolves'. That has suggested the hypothesis that the encounter with the Sultan has been compressed in the legend. In that case we would have a literary reworking of this historic encounter, a symbol of non-violent and unprejudiced courage, a hope that the attitude of the lamb will convert the one whom all regard as a wolf. If this hypothesis were correct, we would have a work of art which combines historical reminiscence with pedagogical aims. Memory becomes encouragement!

IV. Roger Bacon and Ramon Llull

However, this new spirit of St Francis was not expressed immediately in his brotherhood and established itself only here and there. Thus Brother Aegidus of Assisi went to Tunis in quite a different spirit in 1219,[20] and Brother Bernard and his companions to Morocco in 1220. They provoked martyrdom with the most aggressive tones. Aegidus was forcibly sent back to Italy by the Christians living in Tunis, and Bernard and his companions[21] became the first martyrs of the Franciscan community. Following them, many other Franciscans[22] were completely untouched by the spirit described above 'among the Saracens or other unbelievers'.

Over against this aggressive attitude stands the 'non-violent theology' of many Franciscans, the most prominent names among whom are Adam de Mars (died 1259), Roger Bacon (died after 1292), Gilbert of Tournay (died 1288) and Ramon Llull (died 1316). They are all clear opponents of violent conversion and want to extend non-violence in encounters to Tartars, heretics, Jews, pagans and idolaters of any kind.[23]

For example, in his letter to Pope Clement IV,[24] Roger Bacon develops a church political programme on the basis of *sapientia*, as spiritually directed knowledge is still called. And in his wide-ranging *Moralis philosophia*[25] he gives a profound reason for this. A violent conversion or subjection, he says, cannot be successful, since first it is only change and not lasting, and secondly, positions are hardened as a result:

> A community of faith can be convinced of the truth which can alone be found in Christian truth in two ways. Either through miracles, which are above both us and the unbelievers, a way which no one can foresee. Or in that case by a way which is common to both us and them. This way is put at our disposal and the unbelievers will not be able to refuse it. This way is that of rational argument and philosophy, which is also characteristic of unbelievers.[26]

Moreover this approach is then taken further by Ramon Llull,[27] a layman close to the Franciscans. In his *Summary of the Art of Discovering the Truth* and in other works he indefatigably shows how much encounter with Islam means argumentation and working towards conviction. For him there can no longer be proof by authority, but only rational argument. He himself learned Arabic, something which he thinks indispensable for any encounter with the Saracens, and founded an educational establishment on Mallorca, the first pupils in which were

Franciscans. His aim is to found such colleges at which his 'art' can be learned all over the world. His *Book of the Pagan and the Three Wise Men* significantly first appeared in Arabic and only later in Catalan (he translated it himself). Even more significant is the fact that in it he left in the air the decision which of the religions is the true one. In his mystical writings he even seems to be essentially influenced by Sufi mysticism. He appeared all over Europe as a teacher of his 'art', for example at the Sorbonne.

There were also many brothers in the footsteps of Ramon Llull who dreamed the Franciscan dream[28] of an Indian church in what we now call 'Latin America'. Their best known representative is Benhardin of Sahagun.

V. Sufism[29]

Ramon Llull was evidently substantially influenced by Sufi mysticism. We can even assume that Sufism was represented at the court of Sultan Malik-al-Kamil and helped to shape the atmosphere of the court in which the historic encounter between the Sultan and Francis of Assisi took place.[30] It is even believed that we know the name of the spiritual adviser to the Sultan, Fakh al-Din Ibn Ibrahim Farisi (died 1224), who is identified with the 'man of great reputation and age'[31] present at the encounter. Farisi, a member of the Murshidiya order, was a mystic who followed the famous al-Hallaj, crucified in 922 because of his bold sayings about God. One of his pupils attributes the following saying to him:

> Here, see me on the cross . . . Like Jesus I have achieved the pinnacle of the cross . . . Like Jesus I have revealed in public the mystery which the well-to-do, rich and powerful do not know . . . Like Jesus I was put on the same pinnacle: with love I fulfil the same righteousness. Like Jesus on the pinnacle of the cross of love I renew my promise of love.[32]

This is possibly or probably the face of Islam which Francis of Assisi encountered. The name of these Islamic mystics ('Sufi') comes from the rough woollen garment which they wore (*suf* = wool). In such people, if they were in fact at the Sultan's court, must not Francis have necessarily discovered a kind of image of himself: brothers who were already like him to look at, since he himself wore a similar garment?

However, the argument that the mystic Farisi was at the meeting with Francis has been contradicted.[33] No convincing historical argument is possible here. But at all events we can accept Sufism itself as a fact. It developed not least from the encounter with Christianity. Its mysticism is so impressive and fascinating[34] that in the thirteenth century and afterwards it influenced Christianity. Ramon Llull is evidence of this.

What is so striking here is the vision of an Arab-Islamic-Christian confession. An inculturation of the Christ event in an Arab context has already been a historical reality for centuries as a result of certain churches. But in addition in Sufism there is the possibility that inculturation could go considerably further.

Translated by John Bowden

Notes

1. The name derives from an Arab tribe living in the north-west of the Arabian peninsula; in antiquity and later it was transferred by the Byzantines to all Arabs.
2. J. F. Hinnebusch, *The Historia Occidentalis of Jacques de Vitry*, Fribourg CH 1972, 23.
3. Thomas of Celano, *Vita prima* 57 and *Vita Secunda* 30.
4. Cf. A. Fortini, *Francis of Assisi*, New York 1980.
5. Petrus Venerabilis, *Adversus nefandam sectam Saracenorum*, PL 189, 659–719.
6. English translation by P. J. Payer, Medieval Sources in Translation 20, Toronto 1979.
7. Cf. A Rotzetter, 'Kreuzzugskritik und Ablehnung der Feudalordnung in der Gefolgschaft des Franziskus von Assisi', *Wissenschaft und Weisheit* 39, 1976, 42–60.
8. The most convenient edition is in *The Writings of St Francis*, translated by Benen Fahy with introduction and notes by Placid Hermann, London 1964, reprinted in Marion A. Habig (ed.), *St Francis of Assisi, Omnibus of Sources*, Quincy, Ill. 1991, cf. 43f.
9. Cf. the book in which the most important interepretations are collected, A. Moons, *Spirit and Life. A Journal of Contemporary Franciscanism*, Mission in the Franciscan Tradition 6, 1994, which includes the article 'Die missionarische Dimension des Franziskanischen Charismas', *Franziskanische Studien* 66, 1984, 82–90.
10. A. Rotzetter, 'Gott in der Verkündigung des hl. Franz', in E. Covi, *L'esperienza di Dio in Francesco d'Assisi*, Rome 1982, 40–76; developed further in the appendix to *Wunderbar hat er euch erschaffen. Wie Franziskus den Tieren predigt*, Freiburg 1988 and 1998, 74–7.
11. *Writings of St. Francis* (n.7), 46f.
12. Order, ibid., 103f.
13. Cf. the Letter to the Clerics, ibid., 101f.
14. Order, ibid., 107.
15. Letter to the Rulers of the People, ibid., 116.
16. Letter to all Superiors of the Friars Minor, ibid., 113.
17. Letter to the Superiors II, 6f. (this text is not in the *Writings*).

18. *Little Flowers of Francis* 21, in *Writings*, 1348–51.

19. Q. Rughiu, *Gubbio. Guida per la visita ai principali monumenti*, Gubbio 1976, 73.

20. A. Rotzetter, *Aegidius von Assisi. Die Weisheit des Einfachen*, Zurich 1980, 20ff.

21. A. Rotzetter, *Antonius von Padua. Leben und Legenden*, Werl 1995, 9ff.

22. Cf. e.g. A. Rotzetter, 'Fidelis von Sigmaringen. Treue zu Jesus Christus und Verteidigung des Glaubens', in *Im Kreuz ist Leben*, Fribourg CH 1996, 129–59.

23. Cf. A. Rotzetter, 'Kreuzzugskritik' (n.7), 126–33.

24. Letter to Clement IV. Latin text and Italian translation by P. Efrem Bettoni, Milan 1964.

25. Ed. E. Massa, Zurich 1953.

26. '. . . quod dupliciter contingit fieri persuasionem de sectae veritate, quae sola est Christiana; quoniam aut per miracula, quae sunt supra nos et supra infideles, de qua via nullus potest praesumere, aut per viam communem eis et nobis, quae est in potestate nostra et quam non possunt negare, quia vadit per vias humanae ratiocinationis et per vias philosophiae, quae etiam propria est infidelibus' (in id., 195).

27. R. Llull, *Selected Works* (2 vols), Princeton 1985.

28. M. Cayora, *Siembra entre brumas. Utopia franciscana y humanismo renacentista. Una alternativa a la Conquista*, Montevideo 1990; A. Rotzetter, R. Morschel and H. von der Bey (eds.), *Von der Conquista zur Theologie der Befreiung*, Zurich 1993.

29. A. Schimmel, 'Sufismus', in H. Waldenfels (ed.,) *Lexikon der Religionen*, Freiburg 1988, 620–22; Seyd Hossein Nasr (ed.), *Islamic Spirituality* II, World Spirituality Series, New York and London 1991, 3–304.

30. Thus above all the Islamologist L. Massignon, *La Passion d'Ibn Mansur al-Hallaj, martyr mystique de l'Islam* 1–4, Paris 1975, and following him M. Roncaglia, 'San Francesco in Oriente', *Studi Francescani* 50, 1953, 97–106; id., 'Fonte Arabo-Musulmana su San Francesco in Oriente?', *Studi Francescani* 51, 1954, 258f.; G. Basetti Sani, 'Chi era il vecchio famoso che incontro an Francesco a Damietta?', *Studie Francescani* 82, 1985, 209–44.

31. Bonaventura, *Major Life* IX, 8, in Habig (ed.), *St Francis of Assisi*, 704.

32. Quoted in Basetti Sani, 'Chi era il vecchio famoso?' (n.30), 224.

33. J. G. Jeusset, *Dieu est courtoisie. François d'Assise, son Order e l'Islam*, Rennes 1984.

34. Cf. e.g. Maulana Dscheladladdin Rumi, *Von Allem und Vom Einen (Fihi ma fihi)*, translated from the Persian and Arabic by Annemarie Schimmel, Munich 1988.

Crossing Boundaries: Spiritual Journeys in Search of the Sacred

Preliminary Findings for a Book of Interviews

Linda Groff

I. Introduction

This is a very preliminary report on a book of interviews that I have recently begun on people's spiritual journeys – focussing on people who have explored at least two or more different spiritual-religious traditions in their lives. This book of interviews, like this article, will be called *Crossing Boundaries: Spiritual Journeys in Search of the Sacred*.

II. Premises of this study, and why it is important

The context for this study is that we live in an increasingly interdependent world where people increasingly encounter diversity – different races, ethnic groups, cultures *and* religions. The important question for our human future is: How do people deal constructively (or not) with this diversity and integrate it into their lives? And how do people also find what binds and connects them across all this outer diversity?

This study focusses particularly on people's spiritual journeys across two or more different religions: what has motivated people to explore other spiritual-religious traditions, and how have different individuals integrated this diversity into their lives? Also, what can we learn from these spiritual journeys that can help other people deal constructively with religious diversity in our contemporary world?

III. Focus

Many books and accounts have been written in various formats about people's spiritual journeys. Some have been autobiographical or biographical accounts,[1] others have been written as fictional or non-fictional adventure stories focussing on spiritual growth and a spiritual journey,[2] and still others are guide books for people's own spiritual journeys.[3] This collection of interviews will be unique in that it is interviewing only people – well known or not – who have explored at least two or more different spiritual-religious traditions and paths. Questions focus on the paths they have taken, on what motivated them to explore these different traditions – including the underlying questions or themes that motivated their spiritual journey through its different stages, on how they have integrated these explorations of religious diversity into their lives, and on how their spirituality has influenced their work in the world.

These interviews thus focus on a trend that is emerging increasingly in our contemporary, interdependent world, where people are interacting increasingly with diversities of cultures, ethnicities, races *and* religions, creating a need in people somehow to integrate all this diversity into some kind of coherent whole in their lives. These spiritual journeys are thus forerunners of what will increasingly happen in the future, and can give us important insights and guidelines for dealing constructively with what connects us as human beings all over this world, while still honouring the diversity of outer forms that this spirituality takes through our different cultural-religious traditions, as these now play out through the lives of individuals from all different national, racial, ethnic, gender and age backgrounds. Through these interviews people will tell their stories of their spiritual journeys and these stories will speak for themselves.

IV. Questionnaire and sample of people interviewed

A series of open-ended questions have been developed for these interviews. So far over fifteen interviews – of one to one-and-a-half hours each on average – have been taped, and a number of additional new interviews are planned. People from different national, ethnic, racial, gender and age backgrounds are being interviewed. They are also selected because they have an interesting story to tell, dealing with their explorations of religious diversity and spirit, and they have all explored at least two or more different spiritual-religious traditions in their lifetimes.

V. Preliminary findings on people's spiritual journeys: unique stories, underlying models and general characteristics shared in common

In interviewing people about their spiritual journeys, at least three different facets of these journeys seem to be emerging. First, there are unique aspects of each individual's spiritual journey; secondly, there are at least four different models underlying these journeys; and finally, there are characteristics which these interviewees share in common concerning their spiritual journeys.

1. Unique stories and combinations of religions explored in different people's spiritual journeys

First, we can look at how each person's spiritual journey is unique in certain ways – including the particular religions explored and what motivated each person on their spiritual journey and what each person experienced and learned as a result. Some of the different combinations of religions that particular individuals have explored who have been interviewed, or who will soon be interviewed, in the order of their explorations, include:

- People of originally Jewish or Christian backgrounds who have explored Buddhism. The former have sometimes been labelled 'Bu-Jews', and the latter include Christians who have explored aspects of Buddhism through the Society for Buddhist-Christian Studies;
- Buddhists who have explored aspects of Christianity through the Society for Buddhist-Christian Studies, including 'socially-engaged Buddhists';
- An African Muslim who has explored many religious-spiritual traditions and now honours the spirituality in each;
- A former Catholic nun who is now involved with women's spirituality;
- A Quaker who also became a Catholic and is still involved with both religions;
- A Quaker who almost became a Catholic and still honours both traditions, as well as feminism;
- A former Quaker who became involved with an American Indian tradition;
- An agnostic person of Jewish secular heritage who became a New Age leader;

- A Catholic priest, as well as a Catholic monk, who have both explored Hinduism and Buddhism;
- A person raised in Hindu folk traditions who has also explored Christianity, Buddhism and classical Hinduism;
- A person raised Jewish who is now Bah'ai;
- A former Mormon young woman who is now involved with the Goddess religion and wicca;
- A Mennonite who has remained Mennonite, but who has also explored Buddhist, Jewish and Muslim religions;
- A Muslim young woman from Bosnia who lived with a US family with a Christian father and Jewish mother and is committed to return to her country and have friends of different religious backgrounds.
- A Tibetan Buddhist who was also educated by Jesuit Christians; and
- Japanese who are both Shinto and Buddhist and what each religion means to them. It should be noted that these are only a few examples of people interviewed or soon to be interviewed so far. Many other interesting combinations of religions explored by different individuals will no doubt follow in subsequent interviews. Each of these individuals, stories will then speak for itself.

2. Underlying models of the spiritual journey

While everyone's own spiritual journey and story is unique – in terms of the particular sequence of religions explored, the particular motivations behind that journey and what was experienced as a result, and the particular details of their own story – nonetheless, there seem to be at least *four different underlying models* of spiritual journeys taken, in regard to how people relate to their own original religion and then other religions. These models include the following (and no doubt other models as well):

(a) Sometimes people have permanently (so far) left their own spiritual-religious tradition for another one which spoke to them more directly and meaningfully – for whatever reasons.

(b) At other times individuals have explored other traditions without leaving the original religion in which they were raised, but have integrated what they have learned and valued from one or more other religions into their own spiritual tradition, thus enriching their own spiritual-religious life and practice in this way. This sometimes occurs as a result of inter-religious dialogue, where the goal is *not* to create one world religion, *nor* to convert others to one's own religion, but rather to increase understanding *between* different religions, including sharing of spiritual-religious practices, rituals, beliefs, deeper wisdom and speaking from the heart.

(c) Some spiritual seekers have followed a third path of leaving their original religious tradition to explore another tradition in depth, only to discover later that what they sought in the other tradition (and thought was missing in their own original tradition) also existed in their original tradition, leading them back to their religious roots.

An excellent example of this is Westerners who leave their Western religion (whether Judaism or Christianity, primarily) to explore Eastern mystical traditions, only to discover later that the mystical tradition always existed in their Western religion, but was not emphasized and was therefore missed.

Nonetheless, mysticism (as a direct experience of ultimate reality)[4] is truly the root, in some enlightened person or persons, of all great religions, which usually begin with a person who experiences spiritual truths directly, then goes back to share those experiences as best he/she can with others,[5] who become followers and eventually decide to start a new religion, based on the teachings of that enlightened person, even though that person did not always seek or intend to start a new religion themselves. They just wanted to share their love/compassion, wisdom, and the truths they experienced with others.

A number of Westerners have thus discovered mysticism in the East – where it is a more predominant focus of Eastern religion – and then later realized that mysticism also exists at the root of all Western religion(s), and indeed of all religions, leading some people back to an exploration of the mystical roots of their original Western religion, which they can now appreciate and experience more fully, having already explored mysticism within another (non-Western) religious context.

Similarly, increasing numbers of Easterners – who traditionally focussed more on inner peace and meditation as the path to world peace – are also acknowledging the importance of action for social justice, human rights and alleviating poverty in the world, which they are learning more from Westerners, as another component of creating a better world.[6]

(d) A fourth path covers people who have gone beyond any one spiritual-religious tradition or path, are interested in spirituality in general, and often honour and learn from a number of different spiritual-religious traditions. This would often include 'New Age' people, as well as others.

3. Common characteristics of people's spiritual journeys

In addition to the unique aspects of each person's spiritual journey, and the four plus models underlying many aspects of those journeys, there are also certain general characteristics of the spiritual journeys that these interviewees seem to share in common, including the following:

(a) These people are almost always *consciously* on a spiritual path seeking some deeper understanding of spirit and truth. When people leave one religion to explore another, they often (but not always initially) do this *consciously*, looking for something that they did not find in their original religion. Alternatively, just encountering religious diversity in one's life, due to one's life circumstances, can prompt one to re-examine one's own tradition and how it differs from, or is similar to, another religious tradition. What may have once been accepted without question in one's original religion (from authority figures or scriptures) is now examined more *consciously*, by asking questions and seeking answers that must now satisfy a person and ring true to that person *within* themselves.

Indeed, it can be argued that as we all encounter diversity more and more in our interdependent world, we can either block that diversity out and become more intolerant of other traditions (as in fundamentalist or extremist forms that are potentially possible within any religion) or, if individuals are honestly willing to grapple with the difficult questions raised for them as a result of their encounter with religious diversity, we can begin an internal dialogue and struggle within ourselves to seek a deeper understanding of spiritual truths that can encompass and honour that diversity and can acknowledge areas of differences, as well as areas of common ground. Once people reach this stage of consciously asking questions and seeking truth within themselves, there is really no turning back. It is difficult, once consciousness has been awakened, to go back to an unconscious state of blindly accepting truth from others without grounding it in one's own experiences of the truth.

(b) Interviewees have almost always come to realize that total truth does *not* reside in only one religion or one interpretation of one religion. They are thus more open people, but also genuine seekers after truth, meaning, and love/compassion in their lives.[7]

(c) Most individuals interviewed have come to see that different religions arose at different times and in different places and cultural contexts, but that underlying this outer diversity of religious forms lies some deeper spirituality – and mysticism or direct inner experience of ultimate reality, as defined above – which unites all these different spiritual-religious traditions and paths.

(d) A number of these interviewees – but by no means all – are involved in some way in inter-religious, inter-faith, and inter-monastic dialogue, which has tended either to open them up to other spiritual-religious traditions or to reinforce their openness to learning from other traditions.

(e) Everyone's stories and spiritual journeys are authentic and real for them. When people talk about their spiritual journeys, they also speak from their hearts about what is dearest and deepest in their lives, making each person's life story and spiritual journey a fascinating and compelling story with its own integrity and dynamic.

VI. The importance of inter-religious dialogue

One thing is certain: we live in an increasingly interdependent world of great cultural, ethnic *and* religious diversity, and we must somehow learn to live together on this planet in peace, finding what connects us underneath all this outer diversity. Wars have evolved from previous conflicts between states, during the Cold War, to almost entirely internal wars and conflicts between different ethnic groups within countries today. These often have a religious dimension (at least in name). We live in a world of ever more powerful technologies, which can be used for positive (life-affirming) purposes, or for negative (destructive) purposes, which are dangerous to the survival of us all. We must find what binds us together across all this diversity, if we want the earth and humanity to survive and prosper in future. Various efforts at inter-religious, inter-faith and inter-monastic dialogue are thus extremely important in creating bridges of understanding and dialogue today between peoples of diverse backgrounds.

Many of these inter-religious organizations, which have brought people together from different religions, along with people dedicated to peace in its many dimensions (including absence of war and violence, social justice, human rights and responsibilities, women's rights, minority rights, environmental sustainability and inner peace) have also produced declarations on how people of different religions and faiths can co-operate together on various global agendas for peace. Some of these organizations, and the declarations they have produced, include:

- *The Parliament of the World's Religions:* The first Parliament occurred in Chicago in 1893 and was the origin of inter-religious dialogue globally. The Second Parliament occurred in 1993 and produced a declaration 'Towards a Global Ethic (An Initial Declaration)'. Another Parliament is planned for Capetown, South Africa, in autumn 1999.

- *World Conference on Religion and Peace:* Meets periodically and produced the 'Riva del Garde Declaration' in 1994.
- *UNESCO (United Nations Educational, Scientific and Cultural Organization):* Has sponsored three conferences (1993, 1994 and 1998) on Contributions of Religions to a Culture of Peace. The 1994 meeting produced a 'Declaration on Contributions of Religions to a Culture of Peace' and the 1998 meeting produced a draft working paper on 'Religious Education in a Context of Pluralism and Tolerance'.
- *United Religions Initiative:* Inspired by celebrations for the fiftieth anniversary of the United Nations Charter in San Francisco, California, in 1995, Bishop William Swing of the Episcopal Church called for the creation of a United Religions Charter to be signed in the year 2000. Conferences have met every year since 1996, forming committees and working towards this United Religions Charter. URI will also support a Global Cease Fire by the world's religions for the weekend of 31 December 1999 – 2 January 2000.

These are just a few important examples of inter-religious dialogue occurring today on an international level. Just as important are the many examples of inter-religious dialogue occurring on local levels in cities, towns and communities around the world. Indeed, one of the best ways to encourage greater understanding within one's own community is to start an inter-faith dialogue group. Another good way for people to get to know each other is for individuals to pair up (during such meetings) with someone each time that they do not know well and share their spiritual journeys with each other. The key here is to give each person equal time (for example, fifteen to twenty minutes each) to tell their story, while the other person just listens, without judgment or comments, and then they switch. People speak from their heart and the stories are always interesting.[8]

VII. Conclusion

People's spiritual journeys tell us a great deal about the deepest levels of motivation and meaning in a person's life. These particular stories – of people from very diverse backgrounds, who have all explored at least two

or more different spiritual-religious traditions *and* have made sense of
this diversity in their lives – will give us important models and insights
about how we can all deal constructively with diversity (on the deepest
levels of our being) as we enter the twenty-first century in a decidedly
more interdependent world.

Notes

1. For example, Paramahansa Yogananda. *Autobiography of a Yogi*, Los Angeles
1959; John Avedon, *In Exile From the Land of Snows*, New York 1994: His Holiness
the Dalai Lama, *Freedom in Exile: The Autobiography of the Dalai Lama*, New York
1990; and Mary Craig, *Kundun: A Biography of the Family of the Dalai Lama*,
Washington DC 1997.

2. For example, James Redfield, *The Celestine Prophecy*, New York 1994; James
Redfield, *The Tenth Insight,* Old Tappan, NJ 1996; James F. Twyman, *Emissary of
Light: My Adventures with the Secret Peacemakers,* New York 1996; Marlo Morgan,
Mutant Message Down Under, New York 1991.

3. For example, Drew Leder, *Spiritual Passages: Embracing Life's Sacred Journey*,
New York 1997.

4. See, for example, Denise Lardner and John Tully Carmody, *Mysticism:
Holiness East and West*, New York 1996.

5. It must always be remembered that talking about a spiritual experience is not
the same as having one. As Lao-Tsu said: 'The Tao that can be named is not the
Tao.'

6. This is the focus of socially-engaged Buddhism. See, for example, Christopher
S. Queen and Sallie B. King, *Engaged Buddhism: Buddhist Liberation Movements in
Asia*, Albany, NY 1996.

7. Note: Christians focus more on love and Buddhists focus more on compassion,
and while the two terms don't mean exactly the same thing, they are no doubt related
in certain important ways.

8. David Cooperrider, at Case Western University, has developed this technique
for various situations and groups and calls it the Appreciative Inquiry Method. It is
also used at large meetings of the United Religions Initiative (of 200 plus people).

Do Our Difficulties have the Sense of a Communion?

In Memory of Christian de Chergé, Prior of Tibhirine, Algeria

Bruno Chenu

Globalization should not find the Catholic Church lacking. In fact, as Karl Rahner emphasized twenty years ago, the Second Vatican Council saw the awareness and the beginning of the realization of a world church really present in the four corners of the planet. But the transition from a Western church to a world church is so great that we are far from having assessed all its demands and all its effects, whether at the level of reflection or at that of the daily life of the communities. However, we know that the transition is irreversible. It is taking place under our eyes.

Whereas we have been accustomed to experience the universal church as a simple extension of the Roman church through missionary activity, the universal church being in the image of a local Western church, to our amazement we are discovering that now every local church is the image of the universal church: a mixture of populations, cultures and religious sensibilities. We no longer have to travel the world to discover the problem of refugees, of immigrants, of the poor and the excluded. Our microcosm is a good reflection of the macrocosm. The world meets in our local church. International problems become our daily bread.

All of a sudden our view of the church as 'plural unity', 'reconciled diversity', 'communion in difference' is undergoing the test of a harsh dose of realism. How are we to resist all the centripetal forces to offer the face of a coherent church? How are we to honour otherness without juxtaposing experiences which in the end have nothing in common? How are we to save the truth of Christianity from the Charybdis of identical replication and the Scylla of pluralist conformity? The ecclesiology of communion, which is the new theological panacea, must take into account the social, cultural, religious and Christian differences which separate human beings, and too often bring them into opposition. How are we to hold together the necessary unity and the indisputable multiplicity?

In taking up these penetrating questions once again, we shall benefit from the reflections of one of our recent martyrs, Christian de Chergé, prior of Tibhirine in Algeria. All his life he asked himself about the place of Islam in God's plan, about how God looked upon 'the children of Islam'. Since we want to reflect on difference, Brother Christian presents us with a difference which is insurmountable in human eyes, that between Christians and Muslims in the framework of a monotheistic faith. But he ventures to ask a question on this issue which is extremely provocative: 'Do our differences have the sense of a communion?'[1] The development of such an inter-faith mediation can only be fruitful for us as we come up against ecumenical difficulties or cultural strangeness. The greatest difference should allow us to think of the least difference. Starting from the prior of Tibhirine, we can relocate Christian singularity.

I. Do our differences have a sense?

In French at least the word '*sens*' has two possible meanings: it denotes either a 'significance', an intelligible content, or an 'orientation', a direction. In the first case, if difference has a sense, it exercises a kind of sacramental function: it relates to a 'vaster and more secret reality', inaccessible but unique, which allows us to understand the contrasts and even the contradictions that we note in perceived reality. Could God be using the difference to make himself known?

In the second case, the difference invites us to set out, 'to leave ourselves, in order to escape the risk of becoming imprisoned in our differences so that we are no more than the enclosed temple of an idol'. The three monotheistic religions are moved by the vocation of their ancestor Abraham, who had to set out without knowing where he was going. And do not all the roads of believers converge 'on the same inn, where eyes are opened to the sharing of a single loaf full with love for the multitude'?

In his ministry, Jesus was attentive to all those who were not 'as the others'. He himself was seen by his fellow citizens as someone with an intolerable difference: he made himself 'equal to God' (John 5.18). Yet he claimed to gather all God's children in this difference (John 17.21). This is a gathering which does not kill diversity: 'In my Father's house there are many mansions' (John 14.2). To be the church is to see oneself invited constantly to enlarge the space of one's heart by discerning the traces of the Spirit. Islam, with the words of the Qur'an, offers itself as a difference which needs to be examined.

Is there not a 'right to difference'? This multiple difference 'cannot leave us indifferent'; it destines every believer 'to welcome the multitude of men and women as so many unique brothers and sisters, to be loved to the point of the original bond that each has with the Master of all life'.

For Christian de Chergé, diversity is a basic characteristic of creation. The person who is 'like' is different, and such persons are not constituted just by any fingerprints. Genesis proclaims this infinite variety of the created world with a series of plurals: the waters, the lights, the birds, the plants.

However, it is the oneness of God which is the source of all this diversity. The difference is that God is One. 'He has no like, no equal, no origin, no companion, no associate.' 'God alone is One, God alone.' One explanation of the fact that Christians and Muslims proclaim this oneness differently is a shared inability to embrace God in a single perspective, but even more important is the rooting of God in all difference. 'To see things differently does not mean that one does not see the same things . . . To speak of God differently is not to speak of another God.' We must be careful not to denounce too quickly as impious any other approach to the divine difference than our own.

If God alone is one, he was willed a human being 'in his image, according to his likeness.' So human beings are in the likeness of the differences of God. They are beings apart, capable of signifying the One. 'The human community fulfils itself by sharing the difference which expresses God.' The vocation of being human is the proclamation of the glory of the one God within a community of brothers and sisters.

These remarks by the prior of Tibhirine fit perfectly with the shift of contemporary awareness which has made the other and difference major intellectual and existential categories. The unification of the world by economic and financial channels and by channels of information goes along with a revaluation of the particular, whether cultural or spiritual. In a remarkably prophetic article written as early as January 1968, Michel de Certeau risked making an 'apologia for difference',[2] in the very name of the Christian mystery. For he noted many ways of being within the Christian community, in the relationship between believers and of believers with God.

However, Christians hardly welcome difference with good cheer. Behind 'difference' they often understand 'division', 'rupture', 'strangeness', if not 'immorality': all intolerable situations in their view. A large part of church history has consisted in bringing the other back into the fold. The new feature of the present time is the recognition of the other as other and the emphasis on the other's particularity. The challenge is to convert a pernicious fear of difference into delight in a difference which enriches.

As Christian de Chergé has emphasized, a true theology of creation allows a positive appreciation of difference. The Creator proceeded by progressive separations in Genesis, and human beings are structurally different and have individuality. God made a covenant in Adam and Noah with what Monsignor Claverie has called a 'plural humanity', fashioning it through his word and spirit. 'Human beings are drawn from the ground, and it is from the earth that Adam was created. In his great wisdom the Lord distinguished them and made them go in different ways' (Sirach 33.10–11).

Does the coming of the divine Word in the flesh mark the end of plurality for the benefit of a monolithic truth: 'One God, one people, one church'? Contemporary work on the New Testament has allowed us to rediscover the presence of diversity in the apostolic witness. The canon is certainly a defined space, but the space is sufficiently large to make room for a plurality of perspectives, languages and situations. The Christian experience does not derive from a skilfully developed doctrine, but from the encounter with a person whose stamp on history is expressed in different ways. There is no magic formula, no imposed norm to reduce the four Gospels to one. Their attitude towards the Jewish Law separates Matthew and Mark. Paul (Rom. 3.27) and James (2.24) do not agree on the central issue of the relationship between faith and works. The Synoptics and John do not give the same date for the passion of Christ. Paul attaches virtually no importance to the earthly life of Jesus. The eschatology of the Gospel of John has virtually nothing in common with the eschatology of the Apocalypse. There is no need to extend the list; the canon is a kind of 'canonization of the diversity of Christianity', as James D. G. Dunn has put it.

Similarly, we have again become aware of the cultural, liturgical, canonical and theological diversity which has run through the history of the church. We have not stopped meditating on the significance of a remark of St Irenaeus about the question of Easter: 'The difference in the fast confirms the agreement of faith.'[3] And St Augustine can only conceive of the church with the finery of a glistening diversity, leaving it to love to weave the links between the differences. If uniformity is going to override Christian freedom, we must never forget that the liturgical diversity which remains has always been more attractive than a panoply of rites: a certain image of God and of the relationship with God, a face of Christ, a conception of the church.[4] And the Catholic Church has always had an East, even when it was becoming polarized on its West. Down the centuries the church has been polyphonic.

Certainly there are limits to the hospitality that the church offers to multiplicity. Respect for the other cannot silence a concern for the truth and the aim of unity. However, we could speak of a hierarchy of differences in ecclesial life. In the nineteenth century the only difference that Johann-Adam Möhler recognized was the difference that is incompatible with ecclesial polyphony. False notes excluded themselves as a matter of course. For the risk of the fragmentation of the church is not utopian, as history bears witness. That is why the last word of the Christian is not 'difference' but 'coherence', 'harmony': in a word, 'communion'.

II. The sense of a communion?

Taking up the thread of Christian de Chergé's article where we left it, we note that the Prior of Tibhirine does not hesitate to speak bluntly of unity. The One appeals simultaneously to unity between human beings and union with God. The two appeals are one for Jesus. And all monotheisms have discovered that 'the religion of the One is the religion of love'.

Unfortunately human beings have become wolves to one another. And human history recounts the endless litany of hates and wars, including religion. The supreme corruption is idolatry, negation of the One. It has to be acknowledged that the Christian community has not been able to bear an incontestable witness to love down the centuries, so much so that the division of Christians 'has served as an apologetic argument in favour of the authenticity of the Qur'an'.

So at the invitation of the prophet Muhammad Christians must return to unity, dedicating themselves totally to the One. As John the Elder demands: 'Little children, beware of idols!' (I John 5.21). And the Qur'an goes so far as wanting an agreement about this: 'People of the book, let us come to an agreement; that we will worship none but God, that we will associate none with Him, and that none of us shall set up mortals as gods besides Him' (3.64)

If an agreement is possible, it is because God wants to bring all human beings together. The three monotheisms create community. For Christians, the church is a gathering in response. For Muslims, Friday is the 'day of assembly'. And all want to prefigure the assembly of the elect at the end of time. For 'God wills that all should be saved' (I Tim. 2.4). It is the ambition of every great religion to bring together the whole of humanity. The unity willed by God also seems to be well 'differentiated'. We have no other resource than to live our time in hope, trying to 'press on to the same goal' (Phil. 3.14). In this common goal each can find riches and dynamism. For the sharing of a hope, the journey towards an 'ever greater' truth, are no small thing: they create authentic bonds.

The final community, 'the unity still hidden', must bring about a 'spiritual emulation' 'within the very heart of difference recognized and accepted'. And it is this love of neighbour which makes visible this communion in the making. There is no question of minimizing the difference. Christian de Chergé dares to write: 'One does not compromise unity by denying this difference.' But the difference must not be absolutized either. The differences come from unity; they originate in God. For God is relationship in the Holy Spirit.

Finally, 'the other contributes towards directing me towards the mystery because what he says about it sounds right, even if his approach is by ways which cannot be reconciled with ours'. Here is an invitation to relocate the difference in the mystery of the One. The Christian knows that Muslims are present in the recapitulation of all things in Christ. And for their part Muslims want 'a settling of the differences' with the people of the Book and even with all men of good will. So God has prepared a communion which surpasses human forces, a communion made up of 'many mansions' (John 14.2). The responsibility of human beings is to offer signs of this now. 'It is in fact important that what belongs to the eternal present of God should be signified in the human present.' The communion of saints calls for 'the quasi-sacrament of a confident agreement between us now'. All believers find themselves in a solidarity and a shared responsibility, which is at the service of justice and peace. But also in prayer: 'There is a taste of an authentic communion in integrated differences, a polyphonic celebration of innumerable marvels and mercies in which the One of all our likenesses has left his inimitable mark.' 'Without waiting for the end of time, God can open up other ways of access to his mystery in which our differences are unfolded.'

In its very audacity, Christian de Chergé's hope may seem to us to be completely utopian. However, it obliges us once again to take up certain basic Christian convictions which are illuminating for our being the church today: the unity of origin and the goal of humanity; the unity attested by the New Testament; the ecclesiology of communion. Just as there is a right to differ, so there is a right of communion.

There is nothing more traditional in the teaching of the Catholic Church than the affirmation of the human race. But its current scope needs to be assessed. John Paul II took this up when meditating on the significance of the meeting at Assisi (27 October 1986).[5] He then emphasized the radical unity of the human race which derives from its origin: every human being is in the divine plan. And the pope affirmed: 'The differences are a less important element than the unity, which, by contrast, is radical, fundamental and determinative.'

Thus he took up the philosophical reflection which argues that the difference is only secondary reality, manifesting the riches of an initial unity. The difference always relates to a previous, more profound, reality or unity. The mystics think the same. Thomas Merton declares, in the context of interreligious dialogue, that 'What he leads us to rediscover is our original unity. We must become what we are already.'[6]

And, in Christianity, the original unity relates to the final unity. According to Christian faith, God has only one goal: for humankind to be saved by the reconciliation of all men and women in Christ, so that humanity becomes one Christ. In this perspective, 'the Holy Spirit gives to all, in a way which God knows, the possibility of being associated with the paschal mystery'.[7]

John Paul considers the differences and the divergences, 'even religious divergences', which are insurmountable from a human perspective, marked by sin, as a 'human fact' which must be transcended. We may no longer act as if Christ was not 'united in a way with all human beings'[8].

It is a hindrance that the Christian church has appeared to institutionalize its difference, breaking with Judaism and setting up internal regulatory mechanisms which could lead to the exclusion of deviants. Is unity to be had at the price of uniformity? I must confess that, whatever the diversity that I have mentioned, the New Testament has a centre: the person of Jesus, the crucified and risen man, the giver of the Spirit. The inalienable heart of Christianity, the inextinguishable source of its unity, is the confession of Easter and Pentecost. The canon is also the canonization of unity. But this confession always goes beyond the words in which it tries to express itself.

Bearing witness to the mission of the Word and the Spirit in history, Christians think that they can thus serve the unique plan of God, which concerns all men and women. They want only to name the truth of the human experience in its relationship to the divine source. Their sole claim is to denote rather more precisely the coming of God in human time and to behave accordingly. For them Jesus remains the one who reveals the right relation with God and the right relation between human beings. And everyone can see that the truth about human beings cheerfully crosses the barriers of cultures, societies and religions. It is no coincidence that it is the dictators who claim that human rights are not universal. All those who are persecuted know in their flesh the essential components of human dignity.

In Christian faith, as James D. G. Dunn put it, 'the centre also determines the circumference'.[9] The body of Christ can only be the body of Christ if it has limits. To keep the unity of the faith, the primitive church was to promote different types of mediations: summaries of the Easter faith; a practice of exchange and mutual verification without fear of polemic; the recognition of authentic charisms; the authority of the scriptures, the practice of baptism and the eucharist; the setting up of the apostolic ministry. Later, there would be more developed creeds, the holding of councils, the development of a tradition of faith, the recognition of primatial centres.

In this way the church was to show itself as a communion: a vertical communion with God and a horizontal communion among believers; the universal communion of the local churches, with the ministers which that presupposes. Here the concept of communion is strictly theological. The history of salvation is totally polarized by communion, for God wants to raise up a humankind in his image. If the church is challenged to brotherhood and sisterhood, it is because it has a vocation to be the earthly icon of trinitarian communion, participation in the very life of God. And this vocation is realized in the most humble community as it celebrates the eucharist. The church rightly repeats the sacrament of the Lord in order to learn and relearn that the sense of human life is communion and service.

But it is not because communion is a gift of God that it does not denote the human task, not only within the church but towards all men and women of good will. The other is always the one who is missing to the church since it can only exist in relationship: not primarily to circumvent the other, but to put him in contact with the personification of the kingdom of God, Christ the Saviour, and thus unify him or her. 'For as many of you as were baptized into Christ have put on Christ. There is neither Jew nor Greek, there is neither slave nor free, there is neither male nor female; for you are all one in Christ Jesus' (Gal. 3.27–28). The Christian faith is not the negation of differences but the relativizing of them in a project of communion. The new creation manifests itself by a brotherhood and sisterhood of love in Christ who is beyond the ethnic and religious distinctions of the old world.

III. In defiance of Catholicity

If the Father's creation is the basis of difference and if Christ's Pasch 'brings together in unity the children of God who have been scattered' (John 1.52), it is the Pentecost of the Spirit which makes it possible to think of difference and communion together.

In fact at Pentecost we have a good sample of the Jewish Diaspora in the list of a dozen peoples to whom Luke adds the mention of Rome. What is announced is already the programme to 'all the nations under the heavens' (Acts 2.5). And the unexpected miracle consists in the fact that each hears in his or her own tongue the wonders of God. It will never be the task of the church to impose a common language. Every culture is 'capable of God' and can welcome the one revelation of God. The difference in languages does not contradict the unity of the message: the mission of the Spirit is rightly to enable the appropriation by all of the Good News of salvation, while guaranteeing the faithfulness of the content. The church is born at Pentecost in a communicative diversity and a plural unity. Babel is reversed.

When the apostle Paul sought a metaphor to express the church, he took care to find an image which expressed both unity and diversity at the same time. This was the theme of the church as 'body of Christ'. The body makes it possible to understand the vital unity of a community which is made up of a diversity of members. 'For as in one body we have many members, and all the members do not have the same function, so we, though many, are one body in Christ, and individually members one of another' (Rom. 12.4–5). Each member has a role and is not interchangeable. But the plurality of charisms has a place in a project of unity: for us to 'attain to the unity of the faith and of the knowledge of the Son of God, to mature manhood, to the measure of the stature of the fullness of Christ' (Eph. 4.13). It is from Christ that the body receives its coherence by the joints of ministries. But it is the Spirit which guarantees the communion of diversity. And it is trust in the Spirit which makes it possible to recognize the grace of God at work in the other who is different. The diversity must serve the unity which is its ultimate goal. And one can say that it is the vigour of the particular contributions that makes up the solidity of the whole.

Thus we find a twofold regulation of diversity: by origin and by goal. If the diversity attests to the fertility of the unity of origin, it is entirely directed towards the final reconciliation, which will be an epiphany of communion. The church finds itself in a position of prophetic sacramentality, where it must set up the sign of a revolutionary communion in which the stranger is received as a friend or the powerful sits beside the poor at the table of sinners.

Protestant and Catholic theologians have recently met over the question: must the unity of the church be made *by* diversity or *in* diversity? Rightly basing himself on Pauline texts, Oscar Cullmann has emphasized the problems of the *by*, thinking that the differences have their own charism which must be respected without going beyond a peaceful coexistence of confessional entities. The Catholic retort is to ask whether the diversity is in fact the foundation and fulfilment of unity. Beyond question, writes Fr de Halleux, it is more correct to see between the two poles of the 'one' and the 'different' the indissociable reciprocity of a dialectical relationship in which each conditions the other.[10] The Christian paradox is rightly that unity grows with diversity and that diversity embellishes unity.

I would say that present-day experience in the churches invites us to hold diversity and unity, difference and communion in tension. In history the tension is constantly reactivated by the authoritarian behaviour of some and the hasty initiatives of others. We must endure the tension as the way towards a great truth, and make it fruitful at the price of the changes that are necessary. Initially the first Christians lived in tension with the Jewish religion, and this tension still runs through our Christian identity. At present we are aware of the cultural tension which arises from the encounter of Christian groups coming from different geographical areas. To recognize the tension impels us to imagine new strategies of communication between individuals and societies, echoes of different experiences, for a mutual conversation and verification.

We cannot in fact progress in communion without playing the communication card. The church cannot be satisfied with the juxtaposition of chapels, the addition of rites. It abhors the restrictions caused by the sects. The fire of Pentecost does not keep people shut up in the house but opens them up to the outside world, creates bonds, and aspires to propagate itself. And when words remain barriers between Christians, it is necessary to find gestures, movements, music which allow relationship. What takes place among young people on the World Youth Days or in the Taizé meetings is instructive. Christian identity is given a network of relationships to the degree that it lives out the practice of the twofold commandment, the twofold summary of relations to the other.

Basically, today we are in search of a new way of expressing Catholicity. Different patterns have followed each other in history: a concern for orthodoxy, identification with the Roman empire, a sense of world mission. The most urgent need today is for a redoubling of dialogue, of exchange, of the capacity for intercultural relations. Such a strategy clearly presupposes that the interlocutors are recognized as subjects, partners, bringing about a legitimate inculturation of the church. It also presupposes that each has deep down a desire for communion which makes them sense in the other the same aspiration, even if the distance between human and spiritual experiences is enormous. Life in the church always includes a kind of bet on the other. I dare to believe that my different brother or sister, in his or her own way, is led by the same desire, the same passion, the same objective: the worship of the God of Jesus Christ and the service of brothers and sisters, the coming of the kingdom of God. And already it is granted to me, thanks to the other, to discover new dimensions of the Christian mystery. What would Christian theology be today without the appearance of contextual theologies? We each receive the faith which feeds us because we have placed a bet on brotherly and sisterly love. And the mutual recognition creates, in Christianity, a mutual inclusion. We must constantly be nagged by the question, 'Does my difference contain a desire for communion?'

Because I have raised the question of the church from the encounter between Christians and Muslims, I can find no better conclusion than these few words from an Algerian Muslim, a friend of the monks of Notre Dame de l'Atlas: 'Time requires us today to live out the differences as bridges of encounter, to live out the divergences as so many occasions for brotherly debate and dialogue which are serene, objective and respectful. We also have to open ourselves in order to discover ourselves and to offer ourselves in order to be able to be welcoming.'[11]

Translated by John Bowden

Notes

1. Text published in *La Lettre de Ligugé* 227, 1984–5, 21–37 and 228, 1984–6, 25–42. Reprinted in Christian de Chergé, *L'invincible espérance*, Paris 1997, 109–66. Quotations for which no references are given here come from this text.

2. *Etudes*, January 1968, 81–106.

3. In Eusebius of Caesarea, *Ecclesiastical History* V, 23, 13.

4. See Jean-Marie Tillard, 'Theological Pluralism and the Mystery of the Church', *Concilium* 171, 1984, 62–73.

5. Speech to the cardinals and to the Curia, 22 December 1986, *DC* 1933, 1987, 133–6.

6. The *Asian Journal of Thomas Merton*, New York 1973.

7. *Gaudium et Spes* 22.

8. Ibid.

9. *Unity and Diversity in the New Testament*, London and Philadelphia 1977, 379.

10. 'L'unité' par la diversité'? A propos d'un ouvrage recent', *NRT* 109, 1987, 877.

11. Dahmane Belaid, Lettre au Superieur du Monastère d'Aiguebelle, 17 November 1997.

Contributors

FELIX WILFRED was born in Tamilnadu, India in 1948. He is professor in the School of Philosophy and Religious Thought, State University of Madras, India. He has taught, as visiting professor, in the universities of Nijmegen, Münster, Frankfurt am Main and Ateneo de Manila. He was also a member of the International Theological Commission of Vatican. He has been president of the Indian Theological Association and Secretary of the Theological Commission of FABC. He is a member of the Board of Editors of *Concilium*. His researches and field-studies today cut across many disciplines in humanities and social sciences. Among his publications in the field of theology are: *From the Dusty Soil. Reinterpretation of Christianity* (1995); *Beyond Settled Foundations. The Journey of Indian Theology* (1993); *Sunset in the East? Asian Challenges and Christian Involvement* (1991); *Leave the Temple* (1992).

Address: University of Madras, Dept of Christian Studies, Chepauk, Madras, India.

YVES CATTIN is a philosopher and teaches in Clermont-Ferrand. In addition to numerous articles on mediaeval philosophy and the philosophy of religion, his works include: *La Preuve de Dieu. Introduction à la lecture du Proslogion d'Anselme de Canterbury*, Paris 1987; *Court traité de l'existence chrétienne*, Paris 1992; *Images d'Anges au Moyen-Age*, Paris 1999; *Anthropologie et politique. Lectures de Thomas d'Aquin* (forthcoming).

Address: Saignes, 63710 Saint-Nectaire, France.

ALBERT BASTENIER is Professor of Sociology in the Department of Political and Social Sciences in the Catholic University of Louvain. He is also chief editor of *Social Compass*, the international journal of the sociology of religion. His other specialist interests are the sociology of migrations and economic sociology. Recent publications include: *Immi-*

gration et espace public. La controverse de l'intégration (with F. Dassetto), Paris 1993, and 'The Importance of Religious Elements in the Ethnic Consciousness of Moroccan Immigrants in Belgium', in *Multicultural Policies and the States. A Comparison of Two European Societies*, ed. M. Marijello, Utrecht 1998.

Address: Université Catholique de Louvain, Collège Jacques Leclerq, Place Montesquieu/bte 1, B 1348 Louvain-la-Neuve, Belgium.

GREGORY BAUM was born in Berlin in 1923; since 1940 he has lived in Canada. He studied at McMaster University in Hamilton, Ontario; Ohio State University; the University of Fribourg, Switzerland; and the new School for Social Research in New York. He is Professor Emeritus at the Religious Studies Faculty of McGill University, Montreal. He is editor of *The Ecumenist*. His recent books are *Essays in Critical Theology* (1994), *Karl Polanyi on Ethics and Economics* (1996), and *the Church for Others: Protestant Theology in Communist East Germany* (1996).

Address: McGill University, 3520 University Street, Montreal, PQ, H3A 2A7 Canada.

JACQUES AUDINET was born in 1928. He is an emeritus professor of the University of Metz and an honorary professor of the Institut Catholique de Paris, in both of which he was formerly professor of religious education, sociology of religion and practical theology. He has been visiting professor at many universities in Europe and the Americas. He has written many articles and books on religious education and practical theology. His most recent book is *Écrits de Théologie Pratique*, Montreal and Paris 1995.

Address: 67 Rue Custine, 75018 Paris, France.

VIRGIL ELIZONDO was born in San Antonio, Texas, and studied at the Ateneo University and the East Asian Pastoral Institute, Manila, and at the Institut Catholique, Paris. Since 1971 he has been President of the Mexican American Cultural Centre in San Antonio. He has published numerous books and articles and has been on the editorial board of *Concilium, Catequesis Latino Americana* and the *God With Us Cateche-*

tical Series. He does much theological reflection with the grass-roots people in the poor neighbourhoods of the USA.

Address: Mexican Cultural Centre, 3019 W. French P1, PO Box 28185, San Antonio, Texas 78205, USA.

ANANTA KUMAR GIRI has an enduring interest in understanding the contemporary quest for a good life and a dignified society and is currently on the faculty of the Madras Institute of Development Studies, Chennai, India. Two recent books are *Global Transformations: Postmodernity and Beyond*, and *Values, Ethics and Business: Challenges for Education and Management.* She has also written many articles on sociology, anthropology, literary criticism and philosophy.

Address: Madras Institute of Development Studies, 79 Second Main Road, Ghandi Nagar, Adyar, Chennai 600 020, India. Email:ssmids@ren.nic.in

BAS VAN IERSEL was born in Heerlen, The Netherlands, in 1924 and entered the Congregation of the Montfortans in 1944. He was ordained priest in 1950 and studied in Nijmegen and Leuven, gaining his doctorate in theology in 1961. He was first lecturer and later Ordinarius Professor of the Exegesis of the New Testament in Nijmegen from 1960 to 1990 and Rector Magnificus there from 1987 to 1990. He has been involved in many capacities with *Concilium* and the *Tijdschrift voor Theologie*, and is still connected with the Dutch biblical journal *Schrift*. His main publications are: *'Der Sohn' in den synoptischen Jesusworten: Christusbezeichnung der Gemeinde oder Selbstbezeichung Jesu?*, Leiden 1961; *Reading Mark*, Edinburgh 1989; and *Mark, A Reader-Response Commentary*, Sheffield 1998.

Address: Sionsweg 1B, 6525 EA Nijmegen, The Netherlands. Email: bas.van.iersel@wxs.nl

DELORES ALEIXANDRE PARRA is a Sister of the Sacred Heart. She holds degrees in trinlingual biblical philology and in theology; she lectures in sacred scripture at the Comillas Pontifical University of Madrid. She is a member of the editorial boards of the reviews *Sal Terrae* and *Catequistas*. Her published works include *Iniciar en la oración* ('Beginning in Prayer' 1990, translated into Portuguese); *Mujeres en la hora undécima* ('Women at the Eleventh Hour', 1991); *Los Salmos, un libro para orar* (The Psalms, a Book to Pray', 1994, translated into Portuguese); *La fe de los grandes creyentes* ('The Faith of the Great Believers', 1995); *Esat historia es mi historia. Narrasciones biblicas vividas hoy* ('This Story is My Story. Biblical Narratives Experienced Today', 1997).

Address: Manuel Fernández Caballero 1-1° A, 28019 Madrid, Spain.

VIMAL TIRIMANNA was born in 1955 and after completing his college studies joined the Redemptorist Congregation. He studied at the Redemptorist Seminary in Bangalore and was ordained in 1987. He then studied moral theology in Rome, receiving his licentiate and doctorate in moral theology at the Alphonsian Academy. Since 1995 he has been lecturing in moral theology at the National Seminary in Kandy, Sri Lanka, and in 1996 he was elected Provincial Superior of the Redemptorist Fathers there. He has for many years written articles on ornithology for *Loris*, the official journal of the Wildlife and Nature Protection Society of Sri Lanka, and has had many articles published in *Vidyajoti* and elsewhere.

Address: 'Frangipani', 80 Amptiya Road, Kandy, Sri Lanka.

WAYNE TEASDALE is Adjunct Professor at De Paul University and Catholic Theological Union, Chicago. He is a Christian *sannyasi*, or monk in the Indian tradition. He is a trustee of the Parliament of the World's Religions and the Bede Griffiths International Trust. He is a retreat master and spiritual director, and a spiritual writer. His books include *Essays in Mysticism*, Lake Worth, FL 1985, and *Towards a Christian Vedanta*, Bangalore 1987, and with George Cairns he edited *The Community of Religions*, New York 1996.

Address: Catholic Theological Union, 5401 S. Cornell Avenue, Chicago IL 60615, USA.

ANTON ROTZETTER was born in Basel in 1939 and entered the Capuchin Order in 1959; he studied in Freiburg, where he gained his doctorate, and Bonn; between 1978 he created and directed the Institute for Spirituality in Münster. Today he lectures in spirituality in Altdorf, Switzerland. He is the author and editor of more than sixty books, which have been translated into many languages, and countless articles. His books include: *Franz von Assisi. Ein Anfang und was davon bleibt* (1982), *Klara von Assisi. Die erste franziskanische Frau* (1993), *Klara und Franz. Bilder einer Freundschaft* (1993), *Antonius von Padua. Leben und Legenden* (1995), and *Im Kreuz ist Leben* (1996).

Address: Kapuzinerweg 22, CH 6460 Altdorf, Switzerland.

LINDA GROFF is Director of Global Options and Professor of Political Science and Future Studies at California State University in Carson, California. She is active in the World Future Society; World Futures Studies Federation; Society for Intercultural Education, Training, and Research; International Peace Research Association and other organizations. She has been a professor in North America, Europe and Asia and has published many articles in the USA and abroad.

Address: 8160 Manitoba St.,// 315 Playa Del Rey, CA 90293-8640, USA.

MIROSLAV VOLF is Associate Professor of Systematic Theology at Fuller Theological Seminary, Pasadena, California, and teaches Theology and Ethics at Evangelical Theological Faculty, Osijek, former Yugoslavia. He was born in Croatia in 1956 and studied theology and philosophy in his native country, in the United States and Germany. He holds a doctorate in theology from the Protestant Theological Faculty in Tübingen. He has published numerous scholarly articles, mainly on political and economic theology and ecclesiology. His books include *Work in the Spirit. Toward a Theology of Work,* New York 1991, and *Exclusion and Embrace: A Theological Exploration of Identity, Otherness and Reconciliation,* Nashville 1996. He is a member of the PC USA.

Address: Fuller Theological Seminary, School of Theology, 135 North Oakland Ave, Pasadena CA 91182, USA.

BRUNO CHENU is an Assumptionist. He was born in 1942 and has taught in the Catholic Faculty of the University of Lyons since 1972. From 1988 to 1997 he was religious editor-in-chief of the newspaper *La Croix* in Paris. He is a member of the Dombes Group and the French Commission for Justice and Peace. His books include *Dieu est noir* (1977), *L'église au coeur* (1982), *Théologies chrétiens des tiers mondes* (1987), *La trace d'un visage* (1992) and *L'urgence prophétique* (1997).

Address: 10 rue François Ier, 75008 Paris, France.

The editors wish to thank the great number of colleagues who contributed in a most helpful way to the final project for this issue.

G. Baum	Montreal	Canada
V. Berckenbrock	Petrópolis	Brazil
W. Beuken	Leuven	Belgium
J. Ching	Toronto	Canada
C. Duquoc	Lyon	France
E. Dussel	Coyoacán	Mexico
V. Elizondo	San Antonio	America
R. Gibellini	Brescia	Italy
F. Houtart	Louvain-la-Neuve	France
B. van Iersel	Nijmegen	Netherlands
B. Kern	Mainz	Germany
N. Mette	Münster	Germany
A. Pieris	Gonawala-Kelaniya	Sri Lanka
G. Ruggieri	Catania	Italy
P. Schotsmans	Leuven	Belgium
E. Tamez	San José	Costa Rica
C. Theobald	Paris	France
M. Vidal	Madrid	Spain

CONCILIUM

The Theological Journal of the 1990s

Now available from Orbis Books

Founded in 1965 and published five times a year, *Concilium* is a world-wide journal of theology. Its editors and essayists encompass a veritable 'who's who' of theological scholars. Not only the greatest names in Catholic theology, but also exciting new voices from every part of the world, have written for this unique journal.

Concilium exists to promote theological discussion in the spirit of Vatican II, out of which it was born. It is a catholic journal in the widest sense: rooted firmly in the Catholic heritage, open to other Christian traditions and the world's faiths. Each issue of *Concilium* focusses on a theme of crucial importance and the widest possible concern for our time. With contributions from Asia, Africa, North and South America and Europe, *Concilium* truly reflects the multiple facets of the world church.

Now available from Orbis Books, *Concilium* will continue to focus theological debate and to challenge scholars and students alike.

Concilium Subscription Information - outside North America

Individual Annual Subscription (five issues): £25.00

Institution Annual Subscription (five issues): £35.00

Airmail subscriptions: add £10.00

Individual issues: £8.95 each

New subscribers please return this form:
for a two-year subscription, double the appropriate rate

(for individuals)   £25.00   (1/2 years)   . . . .

(for institutions)   £35.00   (1/2 years)   . . . .

Airmail postage
outside Europe +£10.00   (1/2 years)   . . . .

Total . . . .

I wish to subscribe for one/two years as an individual/institution
(delete as appropriate)

Name/Institution . . . .

Address . . . .

. . . .

. . . .

I enclose a cheque for . . . . payable to SCM Press Ltd

Please charge my Access/Visa/Mastercard no. . . . .

Signature . . . . .Expiry Date . . . .

Please return this form to:
SCM PRESS LTD   9 - 17 St Albans Place   London   N1 0NX